INTRODUCING ISSUES WITH OPPOSING VIEWPOINTS®

Organic Food and Farming

Lauri S. Scherer, *Book Editor*

GREENHAVEN PRESS
A part of Gale, Cengage Learning

GALE
CENGAGE Learning®

Farmington Hills, Mich • San Francisco • New York • Waterville, Maine
Meriden, Conn • Mason, Ohio • Chicago

Elizabeth Des Chenes, *Director, Content Strategy*
Cynthia Sanner, *Publisher*
Douglas Dentino, *Manager, New Product*

LIBRARY OF CONGRESS CATALOGING-IN-PUBLICATION DATA

Organic food and farming / Lauri S. Scherer, book editor.
    pages cm. -- (Introducing issues with opposing viewpoints)
  Audience: Grade 9 to 12.
  Includes bibliographical references and index.
  ISBN 978-0-7377-6926-5 (hardcover)
  1. Natural foods--Study and teaching (Secondary) 2. Organic farming--Study and teaching (Secondary) 3. Organic farming--Social aspects. I. Scherer, Lauri S., editor of compilation.
  TX369.O65 2014
  641.3'02--dc23
                                                                    2014001087

Printed in the United States of America
1 2 3 4 5 6 7 18 17 16 15 14

Contents

Chapter 3: What Is the Nature of Organic Food?

Foreword

Indulging in a wide spectrum of ideas, beliefs, and perspectives is a critical cornerstone of democracy. After all, it is often debates over differences of opinion, such as whether to legalize abortion, how to treat prisoners, or when to enact the death penalty, that shape our society and drive it forward. Such diversity of thought is frequently regarded as the hallmark of a healthy and civilized culture. As the Reverend Clifford Schutjer of the First Congregational Church in Mansfield, Ohio, declared in a 2001 sermon, "Surrounding oneself with only like-minded people, restricting what we listen to or read only to what we find agreeable is irresponsible. Refusing to entertain doubts once we make up our minds is a subtle but deadly form of arrogance." With this advice in mind, Introducing Issues with Opposing Viewpoints books aim to open readers' minds to the critically divergent views that comprise our world's most important debates.

Introducing Issues with Opposing Viewpoints simplifies for students the enormous and often overwhelming mass of material now available via print and electronic media. Collected in every volume is an array of opinions that captures the essence of a particular controversy or topic. Introducing Issues with Opposing Viewpoints books embody the spirit of nineteenth-century journalist Charles A. Dana's axiom: "Fight for your opinions, but do not believe that they contain the whole truth, or the only truth." Absorbing such contrasting opinions teaches students to analyze the strength of an argument and compare it to its opposition. From this process readers can inform and strengthen their own opinions, or be exposed to new information that will change their minds. Introducing Issues with Opposing Viewpoints is a mosaic of different voices. The authors are statesmen, pundits, academics, journalists, corporations, and ordinary people who have felt compelled to share their experiences and ideas in a public forum. Their words have been collected from newspapers, journals, books, speeches, interviews, and the Internet, the fastest growing body of opinionated material in the world.

Introducing Issues with Opposing Viewpoints shares many of the well-known features of its critically acclaimed parent series, Opposing Viewpoints. The articles are presented in a pro/con format, allowing readers to absorb divergent perspectives side by side. Active reading questions preface each viewpoint, requiring the student to approach the material thoughtfully and carefully. Useful charts, graphs, and cartoons supplement each article. A thorough introduction provides readers with crucial background on an issue. An annotated bibliography points the reader toward articles, books, and websites that contain additional information on the topic. An appendix of organizations to contact contains a wide variety of charities, nonprofit organizations, political groups, and private enterprises that each hold a position on the issue at hand. Finally, a comprehensive index allows readers to locate content quickly and efficiently.

Introducing Issues with Opposing Viewpoints is also significantly different from Opposing Viewpoints. As the series title implies, its presentation will help introduce students to the concept of opposing viewpoints and learn to use this material to aid in critical writing and debate. The series' four-color, accessible format makes the books attractive and inviting to readers of all levels. In addition, each viewpoint has been carefully edited to maximize a reader's understanding of the content. Short but thorough viewpoints capture the essence of an argument. A substantial, thought-provoking essay question placed at the end of each viewpoint asks the student to further investigate the issues raised in the viewpoint, compare and contrast two authors' arguments, or consider how one might go about forming an opinion on the topic at hand. Each viewpoint contains sidebars that include at-a-glance information and handy statistics. A Facts About section located in the back of the book further supplies students with relevant facts and figures.

Following in the tradition of the Opposing Viewpoints series, Greenhaven Press continues to provide readers with invaluable exposure to the controversial issues that shape our world. As John Stuart Mill once wrote: "The only way in which a human being can make some approach to knowing the whole of a subject is by hearing what can be said about it by persons of every variety of opinion and studying all modes in which it can be looked at by every character of mind. No wise man ever acquired his wisdom in any mode but this." It is to this principle that Introducing Issues with Opposing Viewpoints books are dedicated.

Introduction

As organic food has moved from niche to conventional marketplaces, organic products are found in increasingly mainstream places. Costco sells bulk organic milk, eggs, and cheese, along with clothing made from organic cotton. Target sells organic cotton sheets and launched its own line of organic groceries (called Simply Balanced) in 2013. Walmart, which sells 18 percent of the nation's groceries (more than any other single entity, by a large percentage), also sells organic foods, making it a major source of organic products. But is there a difference between the organic foods and products purchased in supercenters and those sold at small, local organic cooperatives? If there is, what is it—and should consumers care?

At many cooperatives—small, locally owned health stores in which the organic foods movement was born—simply being "organic" is no longer good enough. Many such co-ops judge an organic product in its totality and have much higher standards than simply being produced in a pesticide-free environment. They take into account whether an item originated from a small or large farm; the distance it traveled to reach the store shelf; whether it came from a local, independent merchant; whether it was fairly traded and minimally processed; whether it was grown or produced using sustainable techniques; and whether it was made without causing pain and suffering to animals. Many small organic cooperatives refuse to sell products they feel violate the spirit of these ethical principles, even if those products technically meet the federal government's definition of *organic*.

Other Avenues Food Cooperative in San Francisco, California, for example, will not sell a product simply because it was grown without pesticides. Rather, this small food co-op selects its stock on the basis of the ethical nature of a product's parent company. Other Avenues stops offering organic products should they be purchased by a parent company whose ideals violate the co-op's buying guidelines and mission statement, which embody social justice, sustainability, and cruelty-free values. For example, the Burt's Bees line of natural products was discontinued at Other Avenues when it was purchased by Clorox, because that company conducts itself in ways that are antithetical to the co-op's mission and vision. "[Clorox] is not what we mean when we say organic," says Katherine Saussy, an Other Avenues worker. Similarly, the store stopped carrying New Chapter vitamins and fish oil when Procter & Gamble purchased these natural supplements. "Procter & Gamble's practices are completely opposite our mission and goals,"[1] says Saussy.

In addition, unlike larger, corporate grocery store chains that tend to feature organic products without scrutiny, Other Avenues shoppers are hard-pressed to find organic offerings put out by Kraft Foods (which owns the Boca line of products), Kellogg's (which owns Kashi and Morningstar Farms), PepsiCo (which owns Naked Juice), or other large companies. While these products might feature corn or wheat that has been grown without pesticides, the foods are highly processed and the crops grown on large-scale farms that do not reflect the other values increasingly important to organic shoppers. "We take into consideration the human element of the products we sell," says Saussy. "How they were made, the difference their production made in terms of workers' rights and health. We look not only at whether they are organic but if the product is good for the person, the planet, and the community, in a holistic sense."[2]

In fact, Other Avenues began discontinuing Muir Glen products, a popular organic line of canned tomatoes and sauces, when Muir Glen's parent company—General Mills—actively campaigned against a 2012 California ballot proposition that would have required food manufacturers to state on the label whether their product contained genetically modified ingredients. "It's a tough one, because people need their canned tomatoes," says Saussy. "But the parent company is on the wrong side of the battle, in our opinion."[3] Rainbow Grocery, another food co-op located in San Francisco, took a similar approach; although this cooperative more willingly carries organic products owned by large companies, it ceased promoting any products sold by companies that opposed Proposition 37 because of its belief that genetically modified ingredients have no place in the organic lifestyle.

Rainbow, Other Avenues, and other co-ops view the widespread adoption of organic food as a threat to the entire movement's integrity.

They assert that "Big Organic" compromises the integrity of organic values in exchange for high profits and watered-down standards. Others, however, view the movement of organic products into mainstream marketplaces as a positive development that makes healthier, more natural food available to more people, and at a lower cost. For example, in 2006 when Walmart began selling organic food to its customers, many thought it would help improve Americans' nutrition and health, both of which have become national priorities. As authors Ann Cooper and Kate Adamick point out, "When Wal-Mart adds low-priced organic produce to the shelves of its 3,400 stores across middle and rural America, chemical-free food will instantly be within reach of tens of millions of individuals currently without access to them."[4]

Journalist Corby Kummer agrees. Although initially skeptical of Walmart's organic groceries, Kummer concluded that many organic products sold there rivaled the quality and price of those sold at higher-end health markets like Whole Foods. "In an ideal world, people would buy their food directly from the people who grew or caught it, or grow and catch it themselves. But most people can't do that," writes Kummer in the *Atlantic*. "I'm not sure I'm convinced that the world's largest retailer is set on rebuilding local economies it had a hand in destroying, if not literally, then in effect. But I'm convinced that if it wants to, a ruthlessly well-run mechanism can bring fruits and vegetables back to land where they once flourished, and deliver them to the people who need them most."[5] Kummer, Cooper, and Adamick ultimately think the greater availability of pesticide-free food is something to celebrate, even if not all products live up to the standards of places like Other Avenues.

Whether organic food's foray into the mainstream compromises the organic movement or helps more people get healthier food is one of the key debates in *Introducing Issues with Opposing Viewpoints: Organic Food and Farming*. In this collection of smartly paired articles, readers will consider this and other important issues, such as whether organic food is safer, healthier, or more nutritious than conventionally grown foods; whether it is environmentally friendly; whether it can reduce world hunger and global warming; and whether it is an elitist fad. The wealth of information and perspectives provided in the article pairs will help students form their own opinions about organic food and whether they think it is worth growing, buying, and eating.

Notes

1. Katherine Saussy, personal interview with Lauri S. Scherer, December 4, 2013.
2. Saussy, interview.
3. Saussy, interview.
4. Ann Cooper and Kate Adamick, "An Organic Foods Dilemma: They're Mass-Produced by Agribiz but Better than Eating Poisons," *San Francisco Chronicle,* August 6, 2006. www.sfgate .com/cgi-bin/article.cgi?f=/c/a/2006/08/06/ING9HKAN4G1 .DTL&type=printable.
5. Corby Kummer, "The Great Grocery Smackdown," *Atlantic,* March 1, 2010. www.theatlantic.com/magazine/archive/2010/03 /the-great-grocery-smackdown/307904.

Chapter 1

How Safe Is Organic Food?

Opinions differ on the safety of organic foods.

Viewpoint

1

Eat Organic: It Is Good for Other People's Health

"Synthetic herbicides and pesticides are dangerous to humans and should be avoided. And the best way to avoid putting those chemicals into our surroundings is to buy organically grown foods."

Jason Mark

Organic food is lower in pesticides than conventionally grown food, argues Jason Mark in the following viewpoint. He cites numerous studies that show exposure to the herbicides and pesticides sprayed on conventionally grown food causes numerous health problems, including birth defects, endocrine disruption, lowered IQ, and respiratory disorders. Mark warns that people are exposed to pesticides not only when they eat conventionally grown produce, but also when the chemicals sprayed onto fields seep into the water supply, get into the air, and wind up on their clothing and in their homes. Mark says that switching to organic food can significantly reduce the amount of toxic chemicals in people's bodies. He concludes that organic food and farming are significantly safer than conventionally grown food. Mark is the editor of *Earth Island Journal*, where this viewpoint was originally published.

1. How many pesticide drift incidents make people sick on average in California each year?
2. What did researchers at the University of Washington discover about the children of farmworkers, according to Mark?
3. What does Mark say researcher Lori Cragin discovered about the herbicide atrazine?

I had barely drank my first cup of coffee when I heard the news yesterday morning on NPR—organic food, it turns out, may not be that much healthier for you than industrial food.

The NPR story was based on a new study published in the *Annals of Internal Medicine* which concluded, based on a review of existing studies, that there is no "strong evidence that organic foods are significantly more nutritious than conventional foods." The study, written by researchers at the Stanford School of Medicine, also found that eating organic foods "may reduce exposure to pesticide residues and antibiotic-resistant bacteria."

The interwebs were soon full of headlines talking down the benefits of organic foods. "Stanford Scientists Cast Doubt on Advantages of Organic Meat and Produce," the *NY Times* announced, as reporter Kenneth Chang pointed out that pesticide residues on industrially grown fruits and vegetables are "almost always under the allowed safety limits." CBS news, running the AP story on the Stanford study, informed readers: "Organic food hardly healthier, study suggests."

Organic agriculture advocates were quick with their rebuttals. The Environmental Working Group put out a press release playing up the researchers' findings that organic produce has less pesticide residue. Charles Benbrook, a professor of agriculture at Washington State University and former chief scientist at The Organic Center, wrote a detailed critique. Benbrook noted that the Stanford study didn't include data from the USDA and US EPA about pesticide residue levels. He also pointed out that the researchers' definition of "significantly more nutritious" was a little squishy.

Is this the last word on the nutritional benefits of organic foods? Hardly. As Benbrook said, in the coming years improved measurement methods will hopefully allow for better comparisons of food nutritional quality.

I'll leave it to the PhDs and MDs to fight this out among themselves. As they do, I'll keep buying (and growing) organic foods. Why? Because even if organic foods are not demonstrably better for my health than industrial foods, I know that organics are better for the health of other people—the people who grow our nation's food.

To his credit, NPR's new ag reporter, Dan Charles, was careful to note that organic agriculture "can bring environmental benefit." One of the most important environmental benefits organic agriculture delivers is a boost to public health and safety.

Let's say you're not worried about the relatively small amounts of pesticides that end up on the industrial foods at the supermarket. Well, you should still be concerned about the huge amounts of pesticides that end up in the air and water of farming communities—chemicals that can lead to birth defects, endocrine disruption, and neurological and respiratory problems.

When pesticides are sprayed onto farm fields, they don't just stay in that one place. They seep into the water and waft through the air and accumulate on the shoes and clothes of farm workers. In recent years in California (the country's top ag producer) an average of 37 pesticide drift incidents a year have made people sick. Pesticides also find their way into the homes of farm workers. A study by researchers at the University of Washington found that the children of farm workers have higher exposure to pesticide than other children in the same community. When researchers in Mexico looked into pesticide exposure of farm workers there, they found that 20 percent of field hands "showed acute poisoning."

The health impacts on those workers were serious and included "diverse alterations of the digestive, neurological, respiratory, circulatory, dermatological, renal, and reproductive system." The researchers

When pesticides are sprayed onto farm fields, the author reports, they do not just stay on the crop. They seep into groundwater and waft through the air and are brought home on the clothes of farmworkers; thus, they affect many more people than is generally recognized.

concluded: "there exist health hazards for those farm workers exposed to pesticides, at organic and cellular levels."

There are shelves' worth of studies documenting the health dangers of pesticide exposure. A study published last year found that prenatal exposure to organophosphate pesticides—which are often sprayed on crops and in urban areas to control insects—can lower children's IQ. A follow-up investigation into prenatal pesticide exposure concluded that boys' developing brains appear to be more vulnerable than girls' brains. A study by Colorado State University epidemiologist Lori Cragin found that women who drink water containing low levels of the herbicide atrazine are more likely to have low estrogen levels and irregular menstrual

Pesticide Residue in Conventionally Grown Fruits and Vegetables

Below is a table of conventionally grown fruits and vegetables that were tested by the Environmental Working Group for pesticide residue. The foods are ranked from best to worst ascending and the chart indicates what percentage of that particular fruit or vegetable had pesticides on it and how many pesticides could be detected on each fruit or vegetable. For example, 96.6 percent of peaches had pesticides on them, and 86.6 percent of the peaches had two or more different pesticides on them.

Commodity	Combined score	Percentage of samples tested with detectable pesticides	Average number of pesticides found on a sample	Maximum number of pesticides found on a single sample	Number of pesticides found on the commodity in total
Onions	1	0.2%	0.0	1	2
Avocados	1	1.4%	0.0	1	2
Sweet corn (frozen)	2	3.8%	0.0	1	3
Pineapples	7	7.1%	0.1	2	7
Sweet peas (frozen)	11	22.9%	0.3	2	5
Broccoli	18	28.1%	0.3	3	19
Tomatoes	30	46.9%	0.6	5	16
Grapes (domestic)	46	60.5%	0.9	7	31
Green beans	55	67.6%	1.4	6	35
Carrots	57	81,7%	1.6	6	31
Potatoes	58	81.0%	1.0	4	18
Pears	65	86.2%	1.6	6	33
Strawberries	83	92.3%	2.3	8	38
Apples	96	93.6%	2.8	9	50
Peaches	100	96.6%	3.1	9	42

Taken from: Environmental Working Group, 2007.

cycles; about three-quarters of all US corn fields are treated with atrazine annually. British scientists who examined the health effects of fungicides sprayed on fruits and vegetable crops discovered that 30 out of 37 chemicals studied altered males' hormone production.

I think you get the point: many synthetic herbicides and pesticides are dangerous to humans and should be avoided. And the best way to avoid putting those chemicals into our surroundings is to buy organically grown foods.

Yes, the health benefit to you might be modest. But the health benefits to farming communities, farm workers, their children, and their unborn children can be huge. Reason enough, I think, to look for the organic label.

EVALUATING THE AUTHOR'S ARGUMENTS:

Jason Mark, author of this viewpoint, and Christie Wilcox, author of the following viewpoint, disagree on whether organic food is lower in pesticides than conventionally grown foods. After reading both viewpoints, with which author do you agree on this point? Why? Discuss a particular piece of evidence that swayed you.

Viewpoint

2

Are Lower Pesticide Residues a Good Reason to Buy Organic? Probably Not

"Organic pesticides pose the same health risks as non-organic ones."

Christie Wilcox

Christie Wilcox is a science writer and blogger whose articles have appeared in *Scientific American*, where this viewpoint was originally published. In it she argues that organic food is not lower in pesticides than conventionally grown food. In fact, she says, organic food contains dangerous toxins not even found in conventionally grown food. Wilcox explains that organic farming does not use *no* pesticides, just natural ones—and just because they are natural does not mean they are not harmful. In fact, Wilcox says that some natural pesticides are actually more acutely toxic than synthetic ones; they cause serious health problems and are also bad for the environment. Wilcox concludes that the synthetic pesticides used in conventional farming have many benefits, do not cause serious health problems, and are not necessarily worse than the natural pesticides used on organically grown food.

AS YOU READ, CONSIDER THE FOLLOWING QUESTIONS:
1. What is rotenone, and how does it factor into Wilcox's argument?
2. What health problems have been linked to natural pesticides, according to Wilcox? Name at least three.
3. Why, according to Wilcox, does exposure to synthetic pesticides most likely *not* cause cancer?

A lot of organic supporters are up in arms about the recent Stanford study that found no nutritional benefit to organic foods. Stanford missed the point, they say—it's not about what organic foods have in them, it's what they don't. After all, avoidance of pesticide residues is the #1 reason why people buy organic foods.

Yes, conventional foods have more synthetic pesticide residues than organic ones, on average. And yes, pesticides are dangerous chemicals. But does the science support paying significantly more for organic foods just to avoid synthetic pesticides? No.

A Pesticide Is a Pesticide

I'm not saying that pesticides, herbicides, and insect repellants aren't toxic. I certainly wouldn't recommend drinking cocktails laced with insect-repelling chemicals, for without a doubt, they can be bad for you. Pesticide exposure has been linked to all kinds of diseases and conditions, from neurodegenerative diseases like Parkinson's to cancer. What we do know, though, is that natural isn't synonymous with harmless. As a 2003 review of food safety concluded, "what should be made clear to consumers is that 'organic' does not equal 'safe'."

I've said it before and I'll say it again: there is nothing safe about the chemicals used in organic agriculture. Period. This shouldn't be that shocking—after all, a pesticide is a pesticide. "Virtually all chemicals can be shown to be dangerous at high doses," explain scientists, "and this includes the thousands of natural chemicals that are consumed every day in food but most particularly in fruit and vegetables."

There's a reason we have an abundance of natural pesticides: plants and animals produce tens of thousands of chemicals to try and deter insects and herbivores from eating them. Most of these haven't been tested for their toxic potential, as the Reduced Risk Program of the US Environmental Protection Agency (EPA) applies to synthetic pesticides only. As more research is done into their toxicity, however, we find they are just as bad as synthetic pesticides, sometimes worse. Many natural pesticides have been found to be potential—or serious—health risks, including those used commonly in organic farming.

In head-to-head comparisons, natural pesticides don't fare any better than synthetic ones. When I compared the organic chemicals copper sulfate and pyrethrum to the top synthetics, chlorpyrifos and chlorothalonil, I found that not only were the organic ones more acutely toxic, studies have found that they are more chronically toxic as well, and have higher negative impacts on non-target species. My results match with other scientific comparisons. In their recommendations to Parliament in 1999, the Committee on European Communities noted that copper sulfate, in particular, was far more dangerous than the synthetic alternative. A review of their findings can be seen in the table on the right (from a recent review paper). Similarly, head to head comparisons have found that organic pesticides aren't better for the environment, either.

Organic pesticides pose the same health risks as non-organic ones. No matter what anyone tells you,

	Mancozeb	Copper
Human health		
LD$_{50}$	>5000 mg/kg	50 mg/kg
EPA class	Practically non-toxic	Corrosive and toxic
Health effects	Non-toxic by oral route	Kidney and liver damage
Ecotoxity		
Earthworms	Low toxicity	Very toxic
Birds	Low	Moderately toxic
Small Animals	Non-toxic	Harmful
DT$_{50}$ soil	6–15 days	Non-degradable

organic pesticides don't just disappear. Rotenone is notorious for its lack of degradation, and copper sticks around for a long, long time. Studies have shown that copper sulfate, pyrethrins, and rotenone all can be detected on plants after harvest—for copper sulfate and rotenone, those levels exceeded safe limits. One study found such significant rotenone residues in olives and olive oil to warrant "serious doubts . . . about the safety and healthiness of oils extracted from drupes treated with rotenone." Just like with certain synthetic pesticides, organic pesticide exposure has health implications—a study in Texas found that rotenone exposure correlated to a significantly higher risk of Parkinson's disease. The increased risk due to Rotenone was *five times higher* than the risk posed by the synthetic alternative, chlorpyrifos. Similarly, the FDA has known for a while that chronic exposure to copper sulfate can lead to anemia and liver disease.

So why do we keep hearing that organic foods have fewer pesticide residues? Well, because they have lower levels of *synthetic* pesticide residues. Most of our data on pesticide residues in food comes from surveys like the USDA's Pesticide Data Program (PDP). But while the PDP has been looking at the residues of over 300 pesticides in foods for decades, rotenone and copper sulfate aren't among the usual pesticides

These common household objects and chemicals are toxic or harmful to humans. Clockwise from top left are bathroom and cosmetic chemicals, cigarettes, pesticides, and cleaning chemicals.

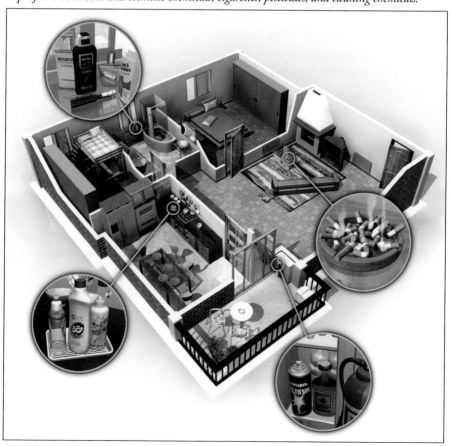

tested for—maybe, because for several organic pesticides, fast, reliable methods for detecting them were only developed recently. And, since there isn't any public data on the use of organic pesticides in organic farming (like there is for conventional farms), we're left guessing what levels of organic pesticides are on and in organic foods.

So, if you're going to worry about pesticides, worry about all of them, organic and synthetic. But, really, should you worry at all?

You Are What You Eat? Maybe Not

We know, quite assuredly, that conventionally produced foods do contain higher levels of synthetic chemicals. But do these residues matter?

While study after study can find pesticide residues on foods, they are almost always well below safety standards. Almost all pesticides detected on foods by the USDA and independent scientific studies are at levels below 1% of the Acceptable Daily Intake (ADI) set by government regulators. This level isn't random—the ADI is based on animal exposure studies in a wide variety of species. First, scientists give animals different amounts of pesticides on a daily basis throughout their lifetimes and monitor those animals for toxic effects. Through this, they determine the highest dose at which no effects can be found. The ADI is then typically set 100 times *lower* than that level. So a typical human exposure that is 1% of the ADI is equivalent to an exposure 10,000 times lower than levels that are safe in animal models.

Systematic reviews of dietary pesticide exposure all come to the same conclusion: that typical dietary exposure to pesticide residues in foods poses minimal risks to humans. As the book *Health Benefits of Organic Food* explains, "while there is some evidence that consuming organic produce will lead to lower exposure of pesticides compared to the consumption of conventional produce, there is no evidence of effect at contemporary concentrations." Or, as a recent review states, "from a practical standpoint, the marginal benefits of reducing human exposure to pesticides in the diet through increased consumption of organic produce appear to be insignificant."

Reviews of the negative health effects of pesticides find that dangerous exposure levels don't come from food. Instead, non-dietary routes make for the vast majority of toxin exposures, in particular the use of pesticides around the home and workplace. A review of the worldwide disease burden caused by chemicals found that 70% can be attributed to air pollution, with acute poisonings and occupational exposures coming in second and third. Similarly, studies have found that indoor air concentrations of pesticides, not the amount on foodstuffs, correlate strongly to the amount of residues found in pregnant women (and even still, there was no strong correlation between exposure and health effects). Similarly, other studies have found that exposures to toxic pyrethroids come primarily from the environment. Children on organic diets routinely had pyrethroids in their systems, and the organic group actually had higher levels of several pyrethroid metabolites than the conventional one. In other words, you have more to fear from your home than from your food.

Your home probably contains more pesticides than you ever imagined. Plastics and paints often contain fungicides to prevent mold—fungi that, by the way, can kill you. Your walls, carpets and floors also contain pesticides. Cleaning products and disinfectants contains pesticides and fungicides so they can do their job. Ever used an exterminator to get rid of mice, termites, fleas or cockroaches? That stuff can linger for months. Step outside your house, and just about everything you touch has come in contact with a pesticide. Insecticides are used in processing, manufacturing, and packaging, not to mention that even grocery stores use pesticides to keep insects and rodents at bay. These chemicals are all around you, every day, fighting off the pests that destroy our buildings and our food. It's not surprising that most pesticide exposures doesn't come from your food.

> # FAST FACT
>
> **According to the Colorado State University Extension in Denver, rotenone is a potent insecticide, sprayed on produce, that is toxic to fish and most mammals. Since rotenone comes from a vine, it is allowed in organic farming.**

That said, there are some studies that have found a link between diet and exposure to specific pesticides, particularly synthetic organophosphorus pesticides. Lu et al. found that switching children from a conventional food diet to an entirely organic one dropped the urinary levels of specific metabolites for malathion and chlorpyrifos to nondetectable levels in a matter of days. But, it's important to note that even the levels they detected during the conventional diet are three orders of magnitude *lower* than the levels needed in animal experiments to cause neurodevelopmental or other adverse health effects.

While it might seem that decreasing exposure to pesticides in any way could only be good for you, toxicologists would differ. Contrary to what you might think, lower exposure isn't necessarily better. It's what's known as hormesis, or a hormetic dose response curve. There is evidence that exposure to most chemicals at doses significantly below danger thresholds, even pesticides, is beneficial when compared to no exposure at all. Why? Perhaps because it kick starts our immune system. Or, perhaps, because pesticides activate beneficial biological pathways. For most chemicals, we simply don't know. What we do know is that data collected from 5000 dose response measurements (abstracted from over 20,000 studies) found that low doses of many supposedly toxic chemicals, metals, pesticides and fungicides either reduced cancer rates below controls or increased longevity or growth in a variety of animals. So while high acute and chronic exposures are bad, the levels we see in food that are well below danger thresholds may even be good for us. This isn't as surprising as you might think—just look at most pharmaceuticals. People take low doses of aspirin daily to improve their heart health, but at high chronic doses, it can cause anything from vomiting to seizures and even death. Similarly, a glass of red wine every day might be good for you. But ten glasses a day? Definitely not.

No Need to Fear

To date, there is no scientific evidence that eating an organic diet leads to better health.

What of all those studies I just mentioned linking pesticides to disorders? Well, exactly *none* of them looked at pesticides from dietary intake and health in people. Instead, they involve people with high occupational exposure (like farmers who spray pesticides) or household exposure (from gardening, etc). Judging the safety of dietary pesticide intake by high exposures is like judging the health impacts of red wine based on alcoholics. A systematic review of the literature found only three studies to date [2012] have looked at clinical outcomes of eating organic—and none found any difference between an organic and conventional diet. My question is: if organic foods are so much healthier, why aren't there any studies that show people on an organic diet are healthier than people eating conventionally grown produce instead?

More to the point, if conventional pesticide residues on food (and not other, high exposure routes) are leading to rampant disease, we should be able to find evidence of the connection in longitudinal epidemiological studies—but we don't. The epidemiological evidence for the danger of pesticide residues simply isn't there.

If dietary exposure to pesticides was a significant factor in cancer rates, we would expect to see that people who eat more conventionally grown fruits and vegetable have higher rates of cancer. But instead, we see the opposite. People who eat more fruits and vegetables have significantly lower incidences of cancers, and those who eat the most are two times less likely to develop cancer than those who eat the least. While high doses of pesticides over time have been linked to cancer in lab animals and *in vitro* studies, "epidemiological studies do not support the idea that synthetic pesticide residues are important for human cancer." Even the exposure to the persistent and villainized pesticide DDT has not been consistently linked to cancer. As a recent review of the literature summarized, "no hard evidence currently exists that toxic hazards such as pesticides have had a major impact on total cancer incidence and mortality, and this is especially true for diet-related exposures."

The closest we have to studying the effects of diet on health are studies looking at farmers. However, farmers in general have high occupational pesticide exposures, and thus it's impossible to tease out occupational versus dietary exposure. Even still, in this high-risk group, studies simply don't find health differences between organic and conventional farmers. A UK study found that conventional farmers were just as healthy as organic ones, though the organic ones were happier. Similarly, while test-tube studies of high levels of pesticides are known to cause reproductive disorders, a comparison of sperm quality from organic and conventional farmers was unable to connect dietary intake of over 40 different pesticides to any kind of reproductive impairment. Instead, the two groups showed no statistical difference in their sperm quality.

In a review of the evidence for choosing organic food, Christine Williams said it simply: "There are virtually no studies of any size that have evaluated the effects of organic v. conventionally-grown foods."

Organic Is an Excuse to Charge More

A 2013 Harris Poll found that most Americans think labeling products as organic simply gives companies the chance to charge more for them. Respondents also did not report a significant difference in taste or freshness between organic and nonorganic products.

Respondents were told: "Please indicate how much you agree or disagree with the following statements."

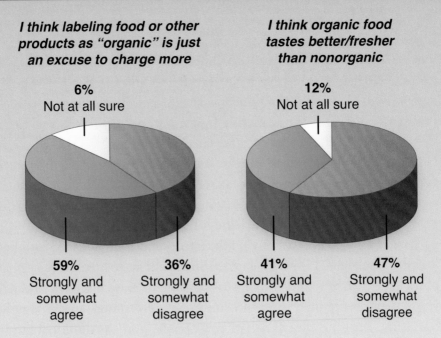

I think labeling food or other products as "organic" is just an excuse to charge more

6%
Not at all sure

59%
Strongly and somewhat agree

36%
Strongly and somewhat disagree

I think organic food tastes better/fresher than nonorganic

12%
Not at all sure

41%
Strongly and somewhat agree

47%
Strongly and somewhat disagree

Note: Percentages may not add up to 100 percent due to rounding.

Taken from: Harris Interactive, March 2013.

Thus, she explains, "conclusions cannot be drawn regarding potentially beneficial or adverse nutritional consequences, to the consumer, of increased consumption of organic food."

"There is currently no evidence to support or refute claims that organic food is safer and thus, healthier, than conventional food, or vice versa. Assertions of such kind are inappropriate and not justified," explain scientists. Neither organic nor conventional food is dangerous to eat, they say, and the constant attention to safety is unwarranted. Worse, it does more harm than good. The scientists chastise the media and industry alike for scaremongering tactics, saying that "the selective and partial presentation of evidence serves no useful purpose and does not promote public health. Rather, it raises fears about unsafe food."

Furthermore, the focus on pesticides is misleading, as pesticide residues are the lowest food hazard when it comes to human health. . . . They conclude that as far as the scientific evidence is concerned, "it seems that other factors, if any, rather than safety aspects speak in favor of organic food."

If you don't want to listen to those people or me, listen to the toxicologists, who study this stuff for a living. When probed about the risk that different toxins pose, over 85% rejected the notion that organic or "natural" products are safer than others. They felt that smoking, sun exposure and mercury were of much higher concern than pesticides. Over 90% agreed that the media does a terrible job of reporting about toxic substances, mostly by overstating the risks. They slammed down hard on non-governmental organizations, too, for overstating risk.

What Is in a Name?

There's good reason we can't detect differences between organic and conventional diets: the labels don't mean that much. Sure, organic farms have to follow a certain set of USDA guidelines, but farm to farm variability is huge for both conventional and organic practices. As a review of organic practices concluded: "variation within organic and conventional farming systems is likely as large as differences between the two systems."

The false dichotomy between conventional and organic isn't just misleading, it's dangerous. Our constant attention to natural versus synthetic only causes fear and distrust, when in actuality, our food has never been safer. Eating less fruits and vegetables due to fear of pesticides or the high price of organics does far more harm to our health than any of the pesticide residues on our food.

Let me be clear about one thing: I'm all for reducing pesticide use. But we can't forget that pesticides are used for a reason, too. We have been reaping the rewards of pesticide use for decades. Higher yields due to less crop destruction. Safer food because of reduced fungal and bacterial contamination. Lower prices as a result of increased supply and longer shelf life. Protection from pests that carry deadly diseases. Invasive species control, saving billions of dollars in damages—and the list goes on. Yes, we need to manage the way we use pesticides, scrutinize the chemicals involved and monitor their effects to ensure safety, and Big Ag (conventional and organic) needs to be kept in check. But without a doubt, our lives have been vastly improved by the chemicals we so quickly villainize.

If we want to achieve the balance between sustainability, production outputs, and health benefits, we have to stop focusing on brand names. Instead of emphasizing labels, we need to look at different farming practices and the chemicals involved and judge them independently of whether they fall under organic standards.

In the meantime, buy fresh, locally farmed produce, whether it's organic or not; if you can talk to the farmers, you'll know exactly what is and isn't on your food. Wash it well, and you'll get rid of most of whatever pesticides are on there, organic or synthetic. And eat lots and lots of fruits and vegetables—if there is anything that will improve your health, it's that.

EVALUATING THE AUTHOR'S ARGUMENTS:

Christie Wilcox quotes from several sources to support the points she makes in this viewpoint. Make a list of everyone she quotes, including their credentials and the nature of their comments. Then analyze her sources—are they credible? Are they well qualified to speak on this subject? What specific points do they support?

Dead Bodies Demand Organic Food Moratorium

David Mastio

> *"The core of organic farming is the rejection of a century's worth of scientific advances."*

In the following viewpoint David Mastio argues that organic food is prone to contamination and contains potentially lethal disease-causing pathogens. Mastio discusses an *E. coli* outbreak at an organic farm, arguing that the outbreak was caused in part by organic farmers' reluctance to employ modern agricultural techniques that keep food safe. Mastio claims that organic farming has misrepresented itself to the general public: Rather than being a small, health-conscious, grassroots industry, it is an enormous enterprise that cares only about the bottom line. Mastio concludes that organic farms need more regulation and oversight to make sure they do not produce food that threatens public health. Mastio is the editorial page editor at the *Washington Times*, a conservative newspaper where this viewpoint was originally published.

AS YOU READ, CONSIDER THE FOLLOWING QUESTIONS:
1. How many people does Mastio say died from tainted produce from an organic farm in Germany?
2. Why, according to Mastio, does organic food cost twice as much as conventionally grown food?
3. How is organic farming like Christian Science, according to Mastio?

Right now, someone nearby is buying organic bean sprouts. It may be the last thing he ever does. Last week's E. coli outbreak in Germany—potentially traced to an organic farm—was more deadly than the largest nuclear disaster of the last quarter-century.

Indeed, in the past two years, two public safety stories have dominated global news headlines—an explosion and oil spill in the Gulf of Mexico and a nuclear power plant meltdown in Japan. Yet in the recent German organic-food-disease outbreak, nearly twice as many people already have died as in the two other industrial disasters combined.

In response to the oil spill, countries all over the world have stopped or curtailed deep-water oil drilling as new safety and environmental regulations are designed and implemented. And ground hasn't been broken on any new nuclear power plant in Europe or the United States since news of the Japanese meltdown broke. Germany is developing plans to mothball its whole nuclear industry.

Yet 23 deaths and more than 1,000 hospitalizations caused by an industrial accident at an organic farm in northern Germany have caused no such newfound caution toward the expansion of that industry. It is easy to understand why. Organic farming has a reputation for being the domain of small-scale family businesses focused on caring for the Earth more than profits. Every organic-produce customer I interviewed at three supermarkets since the German outbreak began have cited better health as a key reason for buying organic food.

That's exactly what the organic industry wants them to think. In a question-and-answer article directed at consumers, the Organic Trade Association says this: "There is mounting evidence at this time to suggest that organically produced foods may be more nutritious. Furthermore, organic foods . . . are spared the application of toxic and persistent insecticides, herbicides, fungicides and fertilizers. Many EPA-approved pesticides were registered long before extensive research linked these chemicals to cancer and other diseases."

If that view of the organic industry was ever true, it has changed over the past 20 years. Organic food has grown into a multibillion-dollar global food enterprise driven by the very same bottom-line pressures that safety advocates blame for Tokyo Power and BP putting their corporate profits before public safety. If you don't believe it, ask yourself why organic bean sprouts cost twice as much as modern bean sprouts. In a word, greed.

The scale of the danger we ignore by pretending organic food isn't a business like every other is nearly unimaginable. According to World Health Organization statistics on E. coli deaths, in just the past two years, more people have been killed by the disease than all fission-related events since the dawn of the nuclear age—even if you include the use

German agricultural and consumer protection minister Ilse Aigner, left, and health minister Daniel Bahr brief the media about the E. coli outbreak at an organic farm in Germany in June 2011.

In 2012 thirty-three people in five were sickened by *E. coli*–contaminated organic spinach.

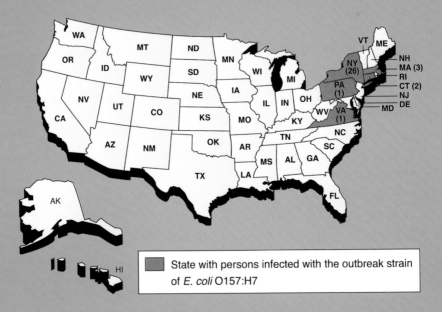

State with persons infected with the outbreak strain of *E. coli* O157:H7

Taken from: Centers for Disease Control and Prevention, December 10, 2012.

of nuclear bombs on Hiroshima and Nagasaki.

The time has come for even the mighty organic lobby to accept the precautionary principle—the idea that it is better to be safe than sorry when it comes to organic farms' potentially deadly practices. Until we know for certain that the outbreak could not have been caused by the suspect organic farm, we must act to protect the public from the unknown risks of organic practices.

First, the Obama administration needs to impose a timeout in the expansion or opening of any new organic farms while regulators and federal safety experts examine the ongoing dangers presented by organic food.

The core of organic farming is the rejection of a century's worth of scientific advances. The same risks that Christian Scientists take with their own children when they reject modern medicine, organic farmers are eager to take with your children when they reject modern agriculture.

Second, before organic farms are allowed to expand again, the industry must prove that ignoring modern technology does not hold hidden risks to public health or the environment. A permitting program for obsolete technology, perhaps as part of the existing agricultural or environmental permitting program, should demand that old technologies outperform new ones at each site where a business proposes to open or expand using obsolete technology.

Third, each obsolete technology should require public health and environmental disaster planning for all foreseeable risks while each organic farm pays into a national fund designed to implement organic farms' disaster plans. Such plans could be accepted only after wide-ranging public comment and the opportunity to strengthen plans through extensive litigation. Afterward, a strict—and independent—inspection regime would be required to keep tough protections in place.

Obviously, the powerful organic industry would object, but the case against it is easily understood. No one would allow an electric utility to build and operate a new nuclear power plant with 1950s-era-technology without proof the design was safer than modern technology. Those who cling to the 1850s feces-based agricultural technology should face the same hurdles. As should those who reject key safety advances such as the *E. coli*–killing practice of irradiating suspect foods and genetic engineering, which holds promise in using natural biological processes to limit the spread of food-borne illness.

Organic farms could be required to take a page from what the Union of Concerned Scientists recently proposed for nuclear power plants. As each new organic facility is proposed and then designed, it

FAST FACT

Scientists at the University of Minnesota found *E. coli* bacteria in 10 percent of organic fruits and vegetables they sampled but in only 2 percent of non-organic produce. They also found salmonella in two organic produce samples but in none of the conventional crops.

should have to prove to an Organic Regulatory Commission (ORC) that it is safer than previously designed organic farms and safer than modern alternatives.

With the lives of children at stake—and the fact that the federal government is taking a larger role in paying for expensive health care—we simply can't allow the organic industry to continue to pretend it is no different from modern agriculture. Have I mentioned saving the children?

EVALUATING THE AUTHOR'S ARGUMENTS:

Viewpoint author David Mastio hinges his argument on an *E. coli* outbreak at an organic farm in Germany. In your opinion, is this event representative of the safety of the organic industry as a whole? Why or why not?

Organic Food Is Not Prone to Contamination or Disease-Causing Pathogens

Kiera Butler

"Organic produce isn't any more or less likely than conventional to carry a scary disease."

Organically grown food is no more likely than conventionally grown food to be contaminated or carry disease-causing pathogens, argues Kiera Butler in the following viewpoint. She cites research that compared pathogen contamination in numerous crops and concluded that the type of crop, rather than the farming method, accounted for whether a food was more likely to be contaminated with *E. coli* (which causes severe sickness, even death). Organic produce is no more likely to carry food-borne bacteria than conventionally farmed produce, says Butler. However, since organic food can become contaminated by pesticides used on conventional crops nearby, Butler recommends washing organic produce before it is eaten anyway. Butler writes about the environment, arts, and culture for the *Columbia*

Journalism Review, *Orion*, *Audubon*, *OnEarth*, *Plenty*, and *Mother Jones*, where this viewpoint was originally published.

AS YOU READ, CONSIDER THE FOLLOWING QUESTIONS:
1. What is a pesticide drift incident, and how does it factor into the author's argument?
2. Why should readers be wary of information that is published by the Hudson Institute, according to Butler?
3. Who is Francisco Diez-Gonzalez, and how does he factor into the viewpoint?

This summer [2012] I've been on a blueberry tear. I buy a little container from the farmers market or supermarket and open it up as soon as I get home, popping the sweet little orbs into my mouth as I'm putting away my groceries. Only occasionally do I give rinsing them more than a passing thought. After all, I usually splurge for the organic kind. How bad could a little chemical-free dirt really be? Do I really have to wash my innocent-looking blueberries?

Crops Can Cross-Contaminate
According to Sonya Lunder, a senior analyst with the Environmental Working Group, the answer is an unequivocal yes, for several reasons. One is what the produce industry refers to as "pesticide drift": The wind can—and frequently does—blow chemicals from nearby conventional fields onto organic crops. Pesticide contamination can also happen in the warehouse, since many produce companies use the same facilities to process organic and conventional products. In that case, companies are supposed to use the label "organically grown" instead of "organic," which can mislead consumers. "The labels are really confusing," Lunder says. "When people say they're transitional organic, there might be traces left in the soil. If you see no-spray, they still might be using synthetic fertilizer, for example."

But the main reason to wash organic produce is to get rid of germs. "Bacterial contamination is huge," Lunder says. You might remember, for example, that one of the culprits in the giant *E. coli* spinach outbreak of 2006 was bagged organic spinach.

Disease Depends on Type of Crop, Not Farming Method

So since organic farmers can't fight germs with chemicals, is their produce more likely to make you sick? In the early 2000s, some news reports said yes. Most quoted Dennis T. Avery and his son Alex, both of the Center for Global Food Issues, a branch of the right-wing think tank the Hudson Institute, whose funders include agribiz giants like Monsanto, ConAgra, and DuPont, as well as ExxonMobil and the Koch Foundation. "For years, organic farming's true believers have made unsubstanti-ated charges against mainstream food," wrote Dennis Avery in a 1999 Hudson Institute piece. "Now they're being equally care-less, ignoring genuine dangers from organic and so-called natu-ral foods."

But Francisco Diez-Gonzalez, a professor of food safety micro-biology at the University of Minnesota's department of food science and nutrition, disagrees. In 2006, he published a study comparing *E. coli* contamination in organic and conventional produce. He con-cluded that the presence of *E. coli* seemed to depend more on the type of produce than whether it had been grown conventionally or organically.

"At this time . . . there is no sufficient evidence either epidemio-logical or scientific, to support the idea that organic produce is most likely to carry foodborne pathogenic bacteria," wrote Diez-Gonzalez in an email. "Despite the apparently logical expectation that if manure is used as one of the predominant fertilizers for organic crops they might be riskier, some factors such as the diver-sity of manure types, the use of composted manure and the fact

The author warns that no matter whether the produce is organically grown or traditionally grown, it is wise to always wash it before eating it.

that even conventional growers also use manure seem to have an impact on finding any differences."

No More Likely to Carry Disease

The takeaway: Since organic produce isn't any more or less likely than conventional to carry a scary disease, and since even organic fruits and veggies might contain traces of pesticides on their skins, always wash it, just like you would any other produce. Of course, rinsing your food won't always remove every single pathogen, Lunder notes, but it's better than nothing. Since running some water over my blueberries will require approximately 15 seconds of my day, I think I can handle it.

EVALUATING THE AUTHOR'S ARGUMENTS:

Kiera Butler, the author of this viewpoint, and David Mastio, author of the previous viewpoint, disagree on the safety of organic food. What evidence does each author provide for his or her perspective? List at least one piece of evidence offered by each author. Then state which piece of evidence you find more compelling, and why.

Organic Food "No Healthier than Conventional"

Martin Hickman

> "When all 162 studies rather than the 55 highest quality ones were taken into account, organic farming was frequently higher in nutrients than conventional produce."

At the time this article was written Martin Hickman was the consumer affairs correspondent at *The Independent* (a British daily newspaper). In the following viewpoint Hickman reports on the results of a research project reviewing scientific studies of the past fifty years into organic and conventional farming. The general conclusion of the study was that food grown by organic methods is no healthier than food grown by conventional methods. Hickman also reports on the objections by organic farmers, who complained that the study dismissed evidence showing that organic food is higher in some nutrients. According to criteria set up for the study, 55 of 162 scientific papers were assessed as high quality. Organic farming supporters criticize the criteria used in the selection. The papers excluded by the criteria show significantly higher levels of beta carotenes and flavonoids in organic food.

AS YOU READ, CONSIDER THE FOLLOWING QUESTIONS:
  1. As stated by the author, who commissioned the study that found no difference between organic and conventional foods?
  2. According to the viewpoint, the study found there was no difference between organic and conventional food in twenty out of twenty-three nutrients. What were the two nutrients in which organic and conventional foods differed?
  3. As stated in the article, what did the study conducted by Carlo Leifert find about the nutrients of organic milk?

Organic food is no healthier than conventional food, according to the world's biggest research project into the issue.

A review of scientific studies for the past 50 years found there were no significant nutritional differences between conventional produce and organic fruit, vegetables, meat and milk.

The findings, intended to answer once and for all a long-running controversy, attack one of the pillars underpinning organic food produced without artificial fertilisers and with higher animal welfare standards: that it is healthier for individuals as well as better for the environment.

However organic farming experts criticised the study carried out by the London School of Hygiene and Tropical Medicine and questioned why it dismissed evidence it gathered that organic food is higher in some nutrients.

The Food Standards Agency commissioned the research to discover whether Britain's £2bn organic industry could claim higher health benefits for its products.

Of 162 scientific papers, researchers found 55 that were high quality and checked them for different minerals and vitamins such as Vitamin C and iron. In "satisfactory quality studies" there was no difference between the organic and non-organic farming in 20 of 23 nutritional categories. Organic was better satisfactory studies, organic food had "statistically higher levels" of phospohorous and acidity, but conventional was higher in nitrates.

Dr Alan Dangour, who led the study, said: "A small number of differences in nutrient content were found to exist between organically and conventionally-produced crops and livestock, but these are unlikely to be of any public health relevance.

"We found broadly that there was no important difference between organic and conventional produce."

The Food Standards Agency stressed that while people bought organic produce for several reasons, it considered that the long-running debate about whether they were more healthy was now over.

Gill Fine, FSA director of dietary health, said: "This study does not mean we should not eat organic food. What it shows is that there is little, if any, nutritional difference between organic and conventionally-produced food and that there is no evidence of additional health benefits from eating organic food."

The result accords with the FSA's previous advice that there was "no significant" health benefit from eating organic produce and also echoes the views expressed by previous Government Defra ministers that the case for organic food being healthier is unproven.

Supporters of organic farming, however, claimed that the results were flawed because of the criteria used to select the most important research.

When all 162 studies rather than the 55 highest quality ones were taken into account, organic farming was frequently higher in nutrients than conventional produce. For instance, beta carotenes were 53 per cent higher and flavanoids 38 per cent higher in organic food than non-organic food.

FAST FACT

The Organic Center compared levels of eleven nutrients in organic foods to those in conventional foods and concluded that the organics were more nutritional in 61 percent of cases.

Peter Melchett, Policy Director at the Soil Association, complained: "The review rejected almost all of the existing studies of comparisons between organic and non-organic nutritional differences. This was because these studies did not meet particular criteria fixed by the London School of Hygiene and Tropical Medicine.

"Although the researchers say that the differences between organic and non-organic food are not 'important', due to the relatively few studies, they report in their analysis that there are higher levels of beneficial nutrients in organic compared to non-organic foods."

A leading academic, Carlo Leifert, professor of ecology at Newcastle University, also attacked the study. Professor Leifert has been con-

A 2013 Harris Poll found that all other things being equal, consumers view organic products as healthier than nonorganic ones.

"I think organic foods are healthier in comparison to nonorganic, but otherwise similar, products."

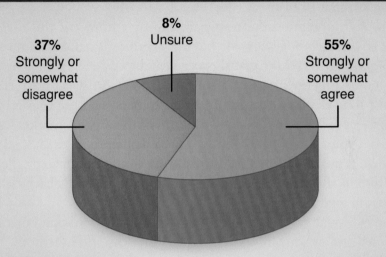

8%
Unsure

37%
Strongly or somewhat disagree

55%
Strongly or somewhat agree

Taken from: Harris Interactive, March 2013.

ducting a £12m four-year EU-funded study. Some initial research, published last year in the *Journal of Science, Agricultural and Food* last year, found that organic milk contained around 60 per cent more antioxidants and beneficial fatty acids than normal milk.

Provisional results from another part of the same study, which has not yet been published, suggests that organic wheat, tomatoes, cabbage, onions and lettuce also had between 10 and 20 per cent more vitamins. Neither have been included in the FSA review.

"With these literature reviews you can influence the outcome by the way that you select the papers that you use for your meta-analysis," Professor Leifert said.

"My feeling—and quite a lot of people think this—is that this is probably the study that delivers what the FSA wanted as an outcome. If you look at the differences they found—a 50 per cent increase in beta carotenes and a 30 per cent increase in flavanoids—they are quite significant differences, and they come to the conclusion that there's no systematic nutritional differences. That's just not very convincing."

During the past decade, sales of organic produce have soared, rising 22 per cent between 2005 and 2007, hitting £2.1bn last year.

Nine out of 10 households buy organic food. Britain has the third biggest market for organic food, after Germany and Italy, though it still only accounts for only 1 per cent of retail sales and 3.5 per cent of British farmland.

Although organic supporters have mostly trumpeted the environment as the biggest reason for buying organic, "quality and taste" is the biggest factor by buyers, shows research.

Britain's biggest organic farmer, Guy Watson, whose Riverford organic food network serves 40,000 customers, said the research was likely to hit his sales nationally. "In terms of the organic market industry as a whole, this is clearly not going to be helpful," he said, adding that he did not believe his veg box scheme would be affected. "People buy from us really for flavour and freshness and secondly because they trust us in a general way."

The National Farmers Union said it had always said that both conventional and organic food to be "equally healthy and nutritious." The NFU said: "It is down to the consumer to choose what kind of food they wish to buy just as it is down to the individual farmer to decide which system he wants to employ—previous research has found there is no evidence to prove organic food is healthier than conventional and we believe there is space in the market for all models of farming to thrive and prosper."

EVALUATING THE AUTHOR'S ARGUMENTS:

The viewpoint author, Martin Hickman, reports on a scientific study led by Alan Dangour that found no difference between organic and conventional foods. Hickman introduces evidence that is contrary to that found by Carlo Leifert. Which expert do you agree with more? Why? What would you need to do to make your evaluation more authoritative?

Organic Food Is Not Healthier than Conventional Food

Marni Soupcoff

Organic food is no healthier than conventionally grown food, argues Marni Soupcoff in the following viewpoint. Soupcoff discusses an influential 2012 study that found no nutritional difference between organic and conventionally raised foods. Soupcoff says the study found a couple of positive, and several neutral, things about organic foods, but nothing that would justify their expense. In Soupcoff's opinion, organic food is just a way for people to feel like they are doing something healthy and natural for themselves—but it is a mistake to see organic food as superior in any significant way to conventionally grown food. She concludes that there is no compelling reason to make organic farming techniques more widespread. Soupcoff is managing editor for blogs at the *Huffington Post Canada*. She previously served as deputy comment editor at Canada's *National Post*, where this viewpoint was originally published.

"What the choice to buy organic comes down to is a squishy, non-scientific desire to feel that what one is eating is wholesome and 'natural,' even though there is no evidence [of] that."

Marni Soupcoff, "It's Official. Organic Food Is a Waste of Cash," *National Post,* September 5, 2012. Reproduced by permission.

AS YOU READ, CONSIDER THE FOLLOWING QUESTIONS:
  1. Who is Beth McMahon, and how does she factor into the author's argument?
  2. What, according to Soupcoff, is an organic purchase the culmination of?
  3. What does Cambridge chemist John Emsley say is a greater danger than global warming?

When a new study by doctors at Stanford University found that organic foods are not any healthier than conventional foods, Canada's organic growers must have been at a loss. What could they possibly say to the dreary news that paying big bucks for organic products actually provides no positive physical or nutritional benefits? Would the growers be humbled or embarrassed? Would they graciously admit the evidence that their products are no better for consumers than the less pricey non-organic varieties?

Well, what do you think? No, the organic growers have chosen to react to the study by ignoring the elephant in the room—the finding that there's no reason to believe organics are safer or more nutritious than conventional foods. Instead, they have rather bizarrely insisted that the study is a vindication of their products.

Here is the topsy turvy conclusion of Beth McMahon, who is executive director of Canadian Organic Growers: "I look at [the study] and I think they found only good things about organic food." Ummm, okay. Not sure how organics' failure to provide any health or food safety advantage is GOOD, but let's follow her reasoning.

Lackluster Findings About Organic Food

From behind her intensely rose-coloured glasses, Ms. McMahon tries to support her assessment by pointing out that the study found that organics reduce people's exposure to pesticides. What she doesn't point out is that the study found the "reduction" insignificant to people's health because the pesticide levels in conventional foods are already so miniscule as to be harmless.

Ms. McMahon further bolsters her glass-half-full view of the study by noting that it did not find that organic foods were any LESS safe than conventional foods—which is hardly a ringing endorsement of her products. What are consumers supposed to think? "Oh, good! This organic food that has been costing me $250 more a month than my regular groceries is no more likely to kill me or my family than the conventional stuff was. I'm so glad I made the switch!"

Organic Food Is "Feel Good" Only

The one point McMahon highlights from the study which is worth noting is that although organic meat is just as likely as conventional meat to be contaminated with bacteria (and the likelihood in both cases is low), when that contamination does occur, the germs found in conventional meats are 33% more likely to be resistant to multiple antibiotics than the germs found in organic meats.

On that small point, organics come out ahead. The problem for the organic industry is that this is truly the only score on which they offer a measurable advantage. And it's an area that the conventional food industry could easily address by adopting a more responsible approach to antibiotic use in feed animals.

Fundamentally, what the choice to buy organic comes down to is a squishy, non-scientific desire to feel that what one is eating is wholesome and "natural," even though there is no evidence that organic food is actually any more of either of those things than the alternative. In most instances, an organic purchase is the culmination of a mild pesticide phobia (most of us have one) and a vague but completely untested (and erroneous) belief that organic food contains more nutrients or less fat or is just simply BETTER.

But it's not.

> **FAST FACT**
>
> According to a 2011 paper published by the American Chemical Society, conventional crops have more protein, chorophyll, beta-carotene, and lycopene—all beneficial to human health—than do organics.

Organic Food Comes at a Steep Price

As the Stanford study shows, organic food is not safer or healthier for individual consumers than conventional food. And it's not better for

The author claims that organic farming is less productive than conventional farming—it produces lower crop yields and does not restore minerals like potassium and phosphorus to the soil the way conventional farming does through its use of inorganic fertilizers.

the environment, either. Organic farming is less productive than conventional farming—it produces lower crop yields and does not restore minerals like potassium and phosphorus to the soil the way conventional farming does through its use of inorganic fertilizers. That means organic farming requires far more land use for a far smaller payoff.

As Ronald Bailey, science correspondent for *Reason* magazine and Reason.com, has argued persuasively, there's far more promise for reducing negative environmental impacts (not to mention effectively feeding the world) with no-till farming and genetically modified crops than there is with organic farming.

Mr. Bailey has quoted Cambridge chemist John Emsley, who said, "The greatest catastrophe that the human race could face this century is not global warming but a global conversion to 'organic farming'—an estimated 2 billion people would perish."

The Disadvantages Are Huge

It's fine if individuals who can afford to pay more for a basket of organic peaches choose to do so because it gives them a pleasant feeling. But the Stanford study should be a reminder that there is no compelling reason to make "going organic" a wider policy objective. The advantages are negligible, if any. On the other hand, the disadvantages are huge. Driving up food prices (particularly for fresh produce) and driving down food supply causes measurable harm to the health and safety of the many around the world who can't afford to indulge fuzzy notions of "natural goodness" just for the heck of it.

In an editorial Wednesday [September 5, 2012], the *Los Angeles Times* expressed its doubts that "the folks at Whole Foods are trembling in their Birkenstocks" as a result of the Stanford study.

I'm sure the *Times* is right. Which is fine. Why shouldn't Whole Foods cater to a wealthy constituency that demands organics? The key is not to confuse that demand with evidence that organic actually means better.

EVALUATING THE AUTHOR'S ARGUMENTS:

Viewpoint author Marni Soupcoff says organic foods make people feel like they are doing something healthy for themselves, but such foods are not actually any healthier for them than conventionally produced food. If you have ever purchased something organic, why did you do so? Because you had proof the product was healthier, or because it made you feel good to buy it? Explain your personal experience with this issue and whether you agree with Soupcoff's assessment of why people buy organic foods.

Chapter 2

Is Organic Farming Good for the Environment?

Organic farmers in Vermont harvest a crop. There are many, differing opinions on whether organic farming is better for the environment than farming using pesticides.

Organic Can Feed the World

Maria Rodale

"Organic agriculture is key . . . to curbing global warming, promoting public health, revitalizing farming communities, and restoring the environment."

In the following viewpoint Maria Rodale argues that organic farming is good for the planet. She says that by not using dangerous chemicals and synthetic pesticides, organic farming keeps toxins out of the soil, air, and water. She explains that organic farming techniques are good for land because they help soil retain moisture and prevent erosion and runoff. Finally, she claims that organic farming techniques can help prevent climate change by pulling carbon out of the air and storing it in the soil. For these reasons and more, she concludes that organic farming is environmentally friendly and should be promoted by governments. Rodale is chief executive officer of Rodale Inc.; the Rodale Institute, a pro-environmental and organic farming institute, was founded by her grandfather, J.I. Rodale.

AS YOU READ, CONSIDER THE FOLLOWING QUESTIONS:
1. List at least three findings from the Farm System Trial.
2. How many pounds of pesticides per person are used in the United States each year, according to Rodale?
3. What percentage of all water pollution does Rodale say agricultural chemicals account for?

Maria Rodale, "Organic Can Feed the World," *Sound Consumer,* September 2012. Reproduced by permission.

Y ou probably buy organic food because you believe it's better for your health and the environment but you also may have heard criticism that "organic cannot feed the world."

Biotech and chemical companies have spent billions of dollars trying to make us think that synthetic fertilizers, pesticides and genetically modified organisms (GMOs) are necessary to feed a growing population. But science indicates otherwise.

There's clear and conclusive scientific data showing organic agriculture is key not only to solving global hunger but also to curbing global warming, promoting public health, revitalizing farming communities, and restoring the environment.

If you do just one thing, make just one conscious choice that can change the world, go organic.

The Truth About Organic Farming

The websites of chemical companies, such as Monsanto, Syngenta and a handful of others that largely control global seed and pesticide production, would have us believe that without GMOs and chemical "crop protection," there will be mass starvation and environmental destruction.

"The world's population is growing," says Monsanto, the world's largest seed and pesticide company, on its website. "To keep up with production farmers will have to produce more food in the next 50 years than in the last 10,000 years combined."

Syngenta, another seed and pesticide giant, boasts, "We develop new, higher yielding seeds and better ways to protect crops from insects, weeds and disease."

The idea that organic farms yield less also comes from chemical companies, who have tested their products on degraded and damaged soil, and barred independent research. Research from the Rodale Institute, however, shows that once soil is restored organically, organic crop yields are comparable to the latest chemical yields.

That's just one finding from a long-running revolutionary research project started in 1981 at the Rodale Institute called the Farm System Trial (FST). The project began by studying the effects of transitioning a farm from chemical to organic methods.

At that time, no university or business would conduct scientific research on organic farming; it was viewed as an inefficient, fringe method of farming. Since then, the FST has produced numerous valuable findings that discredit this belief.

The FST research found that crop yields from organic and synthetic/chemical farms are similar in years of average precipitation.

It also found that organic farm yields are higher than those of chemical farms during droughts and floods, due to stronger root systems

The viewpoint's author, Maria Rodale, published her Organic Manifesto *in 2010. In it she says organic farming can heal the planet and feed the world.*

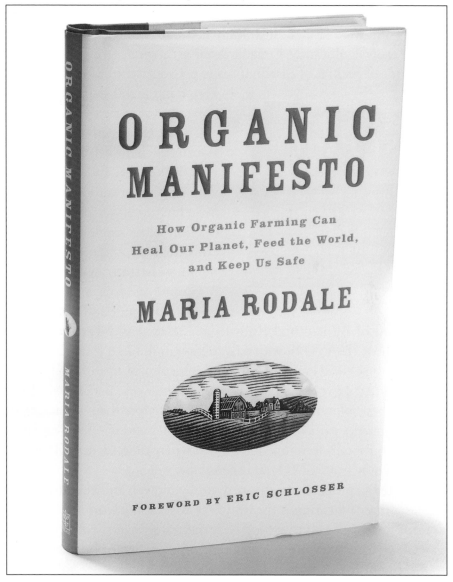

in organic plants, and better moisture retention in the soil, which prevents runoff and erosion.

The FST data also showed that organic production requires 30 percent less energy than chemical production when growing corn and soybeans, that organic farms create jobs because labor inputs are approximately 15 percent higher, and that the net economic return for organic crops is equal to or higher than that for chemically produced crops because upfront costs are lower.

The most surprising FST finding of all has been that organically farmed soil stores a lot of carbon—so much, in fact, that if all the cultivated land in the world were farmed organically it would immediately reduce our climate crisis significantly. Organic farming can pull, on an annual basis, thousands of pounds of carbon dioxide per acre right out of the air and keep it in the soil, adding to its carbon stores year after year.

Conversely, soil farmed using synthetic/chemical methods has very little ability to keep or build vital supplies of carbon in the soil. Switching to all organic food production is the single most critical (and doable) action we can take right now to stop our climate crisis.

FAST FACT

The European Union subsidizes organic farming, in part because it benefits the environment, helps preserve ecosystems, and conserves resources.

Global research also supports these findings. The International Assessment of Agricultural Knowledge, Science and Technology for Development (IAASTD), with $12 million in funding from the World Bank and the United Nation's Food and Agriculture Organization, was an unprecedented survey of agriculture around the world designed to determine the best solutions for feeding the world. More than 400 scientists and 58 countries participated in the proceedings and released a report in 2008, unequivocally recommending a return to traditional, natural farming methods (away from GMOs and chemicals).

Despite the propaganda churned out by biotech and chemical companies, organic farming is the only way to feed the world. Chemicals are not necessary to grow food. Synthetic fertilizers, pesticides and GMOs are necessary only to generate large profits for businesses and to dispose of toxic industrial wastes.

Historically, all agriculture was organic. It wasn't until the Industrial Revolution that we used agriculture as a dumping ground for the enormous quantities of chemical waste that had accumulated.

Transferring our toxic agricultural systems to other countries is sure to bring about a global environmental collapse. The energy required, the toxicity of the chemicals, and the degradation of the soil will be fatal. Instead, we need to export the knowledge we have gained about successful modern organic farming and help others adapt these practices.

Debunking the Myths

If the research is so clear, why haven't more farmers transitioned to organic?

The chemical farmers I've interviewed truly believe they need to increase production because they are on a patriotic mission to feed the world. Chemical and biotech companies spend billions of dollars each year to drive this message home. Yet the problem isn't food scarcity—it's too much food—but fear of famine sure sells chemicals. Our ability to feed ourselves, in fact, is less about production ability and more about politics and instability.

"The world's worst famines are not caused by crop failure; they are caused by faulty political systems that prevent the market from correcting itself," writes Charles Wheelen in his book, "Naked Economics." "Relatively minor agricultural disturbances become catastrophes because imports are not allowed, or prices are not allowed to rise, or farmers are not allowed to grow alternative crops, or politics in some other way interferes with the market's normal ability to correct itself."

The recent global recession greatly increased hunger around the world. A study commissioned by the United Nations concluded that the quantity of food was not the cause—the price of food and political instability were.

Volatile fuel prices and the increased demand for biofuels are among the biggest factors. They led to soaring food prices in 2008 (as much as 24 percent higher than 2007), causing riots in more than 30 countries.

Beyond Feeding the World

The benefits of organic extend far beyond simply being the most effective way to feed the world and mitigate global warming. Organic also is essential for the health of consumers and the environment.

A conservative estimate of current pesticide use in American agriculture is about 1.2 billion pounds a year—about 4 pounds for every person. More than 80,000 new chemical compounds have been introduced since WWII. Many of them are used in agriculture.

Traces of these chemicals can be detected in virtually each and every one of us, yet only half the compounds have been tested, even minimally, and less than 20 percent have been tested for their effects on fetal nervous systems. At least 75 percent of the manufactured chemical compounds that have been tested are known to cause cancer and are toxic to the human brain.

Research links agricultural chemicals and GMOs to asthma, allergies, autism, ADHD, cancer, diabetes, infertility, childhood leukemia, obesity, organ failure, accelerated aging, Parkinson's disease, genital malformations and intestinal damage. Many researchers have found that there is no such thing as a "safe" dose of these chemicals; smaller doses can be just as harmful as high doses.

The effects of chemical agriculture on the environment are equally damaging. Sixty percent of the fresh water in the United States is used for agricultural purposes. When it's used for chemical agriculture, all those chemicals leach through the soil and into the waterways and wells to poison our drinking water, our rivers and streams, our bays and oceans, and, ultimately, all of us.

It has been estimated that it would take an immediate 45 percent reduction in the amount of agricultural chemicals applied to our soils to have any impact at all on slowing the growth of the dead zones in our coastal waters. Agricultural chemicals currently account for approximately two-thirds of all water pollution.

Where Do We Go from Here?

Without government policies that keep chemically produced food artificially cheap, organic food would cost less than chemical food—far less. Yet in Congress' effort to "protect jobs" (mainly at chemical companies) and American farmers, it has put farmers on an economic treadmill. By providing payment incentives to keep growing crops, such as corn and soybeans, chemically, it's challenging to switch to organic or grow other crops.

Government policies encourage the use of GMOs and chemicals, put farmers around the world out of business by lowering export prices, and teach farmers how to work a system that is dysfunctional rather than how to become better farmers, creating a sense of entitlement and codependency that is hard to escape.

Our government needs to turn its policies upside-down and start giving tax breaks to those people and companies that are benefiting people and the planet and finding positive solutions to our food, farming, energy and climate problems. We need to encourage farmers to transition to organic as quickly as possible. We need to reorient the incentives so that the prices of organic foods and agricultural fibers reflect their real costs and are affordable.

We consumers have an important role to play, too. We must demand organic and we must unite. A unified voice is precisely what the environmental/organic movement lacks. When foodies sing the praises of local food sources and don't mention organic, chemical companies are laughing all the way to the bank.

We still have time to heal the planet, feed the world, and keep us all safe. Soil can regenerate. People who eat organic foods reduce their pesticide intake by as much as 90 percent.

Buy organic food. Stop using chemicals and start supporting organic farmers. No other single choice you can make to improve the health of your family and the planet will have greater repercussions for our future.

EVALUATING THE AUTHOR'S ARGUMENTS:

In this viewpoint Maria Rodale says that organic farming can help prevent climate change. But in the following viewpoint Steve Savage says that organic farming contributes to climate change. List the explanation each author offers for his or her perspective. Then state with which author you agree—does organic farming likely contribute to or help prevent climate change? Why?

Six Reasons Organic Is NOT the Most Environmentally Friendly Way to Farm

Steve Savage

"Organic farming is not the best way to farm from an environmental point of view."

In the following viewpoint Steve Savage argues that organic farming is not environmentally friendly, despite popular belief. He argues that even though organic farming uses natural pesticides, many of these are more toxic than synthetic pesticides, which have been designed to reduce environmental harm. Organic farming techniques also emit methane gas, which Savage says contributes to global warming. They also produce less food per acre than conventional farming methods, which Savage says wastes land and resources and cannot be considered environmentally friendly. Savage says organic farming techniques and outputs fail to take advantage of modern technology that has made conventional farming more efficient and environmentally friendly. He

Steve Savage, "Six Reasons Organic is NOT the Most Environmentally Friendly Way to Farm," Applied Mythology.com, April 23, 2013. Reproduced by permission.

concludes that organic farming is not better for the environment and is even worse for it in some ways. Savage is an agricultural scientist. He runs the *Applied Mythology* blog, where this viewpoint was originally published.

AS YOU READ, CONSIDER THE FOLLOWING QUESTIONS:
1. What is a copper-based fungicide, and how does it factor into Savage's argument?
2. What is no-till farming, and what bearing does it have on Savage's argument?
3. In what way does organic farmers' avoidance of synthetic fertilizers hurt the environment, according to the author?

Contrary to widespread consumer belief, organic farming is *not* the best way to farm from an environmental point of view. The guiding principal of organic is to rely exclusively on natural inputs. That was decided early in the 20th century, decades before the scientific disciplines of toxicology, environmental studies and climate science emerged to inform our understanding of how farming practices impact the environment. As both farming and science have progressed, there are now several cutting edge agricultural practices which are good for the environment, but difficult or impossible for organic farmers to implement within the constraints of their pre-scientific rules. . . .

There was one window during which the rules for organic might have been adjusted to reflect a more modern understanding. In 1990 the US Congress charged the USDA with the task of setting a national standard for what products could be legally sold as Organic. That agency was inclined to include more science in a definition of "what is safest for us and for the environment," but the organic community of that day was adamant that the rule should only reflect the purely natural definition embraced by their existing customer base. Long before the final Organic Standards were published in 2002, it was clear that the industry preference had prevailed and that the rules of organic would still reflect their pre-scientific origins. That is why the following six environmental issues exist for organic farming.

1. Less than Optimal Fungicides

Organic farmers use pesticides, but only those qualified as sufficiently natural. Thus, copper-based fungicides are among the few options available to an organic grower for the control of fungal plant diseases. These are high-use rate products that require frequent re-application and which are quite toxic to aquatic invertebrates. There are much more effective, and far less toxic, synthetic fungicide options without environmental issues, and which, unlike copper, break down into completely innocuous materials. Organic growers can't use those fungicides. Similarly there are many environmentally benign, synthetic insecticides and herbicides which cannot be used.

2. A Surprisingly High Carbon Footprint for Compost

The greatest original contribution of the early organic movement was its focus on building soil health. One of the main ways that organic farmers do this is by physically incorporating tons of organic matter into the soil in the form of composts. Unfortunately, during the process of composting a substantial amount of methane is emitted which means that broad use of this soil-building approach would be problematic from a climate change point of view.

3. Practical Barriers to Implementing No-Till Farming

The best approach to building soil quality is minimizing soil disturbance (e.g. no plowing or tilling) combined with the use of cover crops. Such farming systems have multiple environmental advantages, particularly with respect to limiting erosion and nutrient movement into water. Organic growers frequently do plant cover crops, but without effective herbicides, they tend to rely on tillage for weed control. There are efforts underway to find a way to do organic no-till, but they are not really scalable.

4. Difficulties Implementing Optimized Fertilization

Fertilizers are associated with many of the biggest environmental issues for agriculture because of the challenges in supplying all a crop needs without leading to movement of those nutrients into surface or ground water or to emissions of the highly potent greenhouse gas, nitrous oxide. The best practice is to "spoon feed" the nutrients

Soil scientists collect gas emissions from soil. Pesticides cause methane, a greenhouse gas, to be produced in the soil.

through the irrigation system at levels designed to closely track the changing demands of the crop throughout the season.

This requires water-soluble forms of the nutrients and that is very expensive to do for the natural fertilizer sources allowed in organic. Since the plants absorb those nutrients in exactly the same molecular forms regardless of source, this cost barrier is a non-scientific impediment to doing the best thing from an environmental point of view.

Organic fertilizers like composts or manures are also much less practical for variable rate application, an environmentally beneficial option for rain-fed crops in which different amounts of fertilizer are applied to different parts of the field based on geo-referenced soil and yield mapping data. Finally, the organic avoidance of "synthetic fertilizers" would mean that these growers would not be able to use what appear to be promising small-scale, carbon-neutral, renewable energy-driven systems for making nitrogen fertilizers.

5. Lower Land-Use Efficiency

The per-acre yields of organic crops are significantly lower than those for conventional. This has been well documented both by meta-analysis of published research comparisons and by public data generated through USDA commercial production surveys.

The shortfall is driven by limited pesticide options, difficulties in meeting peak fertilizer demand, and in some cases by not being able to use biotech traits. If organic production were used for a significant proportion of crop production, these lower yields would increase the pressure for new land-use-conversion—a serious environmental issue because of the biodiversity and greenhouse gas ramifications.

6. Lack of an Economic Model to Move Beyond Niche Status

Finally, agriculture needs to change in ways that accomplish both productivity and environmental goals. That optimal farming approach must become the dominant system over time. Even if organic had maintained its growth trend from 1995 to 2008, organic acreage in 2050 would still have represented less than 3% of US cropland.

Then, between 2008 and 2011, USDA survey data showed no net gain in US organic acreage. Environmentally desirable "conventional" practices like no-till, cover cropping and a variety of other precision agriculture innovations are already practiced on a much broader scale and have the potential to be economically attractive for farmers without any price premium mechanisms. Innovations in farmland leases could greatly accelerate the conversion process if growers could be guaranteed long-term control of fields so that they could profit from their investments in building soil quality.

Few Switch to Organic Foods for Environmental Reasons

A 2008 Gallup poll found that most people recycled, changed their driving habits, or reduced their energy use in order to live a "greener" life—very few switched to organic foods as part of this effort.

Question: *"What are some of the specific changes you have made in your shopping and living habits to help protect the environment?"*

Change	Percentage
None/nothing	2%
Conserve water	5%
Eat more organic/homegrown foods	**5%**
Use energy-saving ight bulbs	7%
Buy/Use more "green" products	7%
Drive more fuel-efficient car/Maintain car	9%
Use less electricity/Conserve energy	10%
Buy biodegradable products	14%
Drive less/Consolidate trips/Carpool	17%
Recycle/Recycle more	39%
Other	16%
Unsure	12%

Taken from: Gallup poll, March 6–9, 2008.

7. Consumers Who Want to Do the Right Thing

There are many consumers who are willing to spend more for organic food because they believe that they are making a positive difference for the environment. While it is commendable that people are willing to do that, the pre-scientific basis for the organic rules means that the environmental superiority of organic cannot be assumed. While "only natural" is appealing as a marketing message, it is not the best guide for how to farm with minimal environmental impact. Between rigorous, science-based regulation, public and private investments in new technology development, and farmer innovation, modern agriculture has been making excellent environmental progress. That trend, not organic, is what we need to encourage.

EVALUATING THE AUTHOR'S ARGUMENTS:

Both Steve Savage (author of this viewpoint) and Maria Rodale (author of the previous viewpoint) have strong agricultural backgrounds. Research both of these authors and write one paragraph each about their credentials. Given that both have expertise in their field, how do you account for the fact that they disagree with each other? Incorporate the information you learned in your research into your answer.

Organic Farming Conserves Resources

Brian Palmer

"Organic farming uses significantly less energy than conventional."

Organic farming techniques conserve resources, argues Brian Palmer in the following viewpoint. He explains that conventional farming techniques require a lot of energy, such as from nitrogen-based fertilizers. By avoiding these products, says Palmer, organic farming is able to be much less energy intensive. Foods produced by organic farming techniques require much less energy to make, which makes them better for the planet. Palmer says that with farming there are always environmental trade-offs; one technique will save resources in one category but use more in another. Although organic farming may use more land than conventional farming, Palmer says it is more environmentally friendly because of the amount of oil and energy it saves. Palmer writes about health and science for the *Washington Post,* where this viewpoint was originally published.

AS YOU READ, CONSIDER THE FOLLOWING QUESTIONS:
1. How many megajoules of energy does it take to farm one hectare of organic corn, according to Palmer? How many does it take to farm one hectare of conventional corn?
2. What percentage of the energy used in conventional farming can be attributed to nitrogen-based fertilizer?
3. Overall, how much energy (what percentage) does organic farming save per hectare when compared with conventional farming, according to Palmer?

A few weeks ago [in October 2012], after a major study showed that organically grown food offers little or no nutritional benefit over the cheaper, conventionally grown equivalent, I began investigating the other major reason people buy organic: saving the environment.

The environmental impact of a product is too complex to cover comprehensively in a few hundred words, so I began with one aspect of it, land use, and looked at how recently released data shows that conventional farming produces more food on less land than organic farming.

Several organically inclined readers of this column were disappointed with that finding, and a few dismissed it as insignificant in the larger picture of environmental impact. Before moving to other aspects of the ecological analysis, I want to briefly discuss the dangers of that viewpoint.

There Are Always Environmental Trade-Offs

The things we produce are neither wholly good nor wholly bad for the environment. Most of the choices we make involve balancing different kinds of environmental harms. Consider the quandary of paper bags vs. plastic bags. The former require large amounts of water and tree farms on land that could be put to other uses, while the latter involve the extraction of petroleum and take ages to biodegrade. Choosing between the two can seem like a kind of environmental Sophie's choice [an impossibly difficult decision between two things].

The same goes for food. As world population grows and the need for calories grows along with it, the environmental benefits of organic farming won't matter if we have to sacrifice precious acres of biodiversity hot zones and old-growth forest to organic farms.

Organic Farming Avoids Energy-Intensive Fertilizer

Let's move on to energy use. Although the data are incomplete, most studies suggest that organic farming uses significantly less energy than conventional.

The Rodale Institute, which promotes organic farming, has been investigating this question for more than 30 years. It grows organic and conventional corn, wheat and soy side by side on test plots and measures the energy inputs for each. According to the nonprofit organization's numbers, farming one hectare (about 2.5 acres) of organic corn requires 10,150 megajoules of energy. (That's the approximate

The Rodale Institute farm in Kutztown, Pennsylvania, promotes organic farming. It grows organic and conventional corn, wheat, and soybeans side by side on test plots and measures the energy inputs for each.

amount of energy in 78 gallons of gasoline.) By contrast, one hectare of conventionally grown corn requires 17,372 megajoules, 71 percent more than the organic crop.

What accounts for this enormous difference? It's not the pesticides and herbicides that some consumers are most concerned about. Rather, it's nitrogen-based fertilizer, which represents 41 percent of the energy used in the conventional technique.

"Corn is a heavy feeder, and conventional farmers have to pound their plots with nitrogen," says Mark Smallwood, executive director of the Rodale Institute. "The manufacture and transport of synthetic nitrogen requires a tremendous amount of oil."

Pesticides and Herbicides Take Energy, Too

Organic corn requires nitrogen as well, but it comes from less energy-intensive sources. Some nitrogen comes from the composted manure of dairy and beef cattle. The only environmental impact of the manure is the diesel required to bring it to the farm, because environmental analysts allocate the other energy inputs required to make manure—including feed for the livestock—to the cows' intended products, such as milk and beef. Organic farmers also use nitrogen-fixing cover crops such as legumes, which not only add nitrogen to the soil but also provide legumes to our grocery stores.

So what about those pesticides and herbicides? From an energy standpoint, they're not as significant as the fertilizer. Synthetic herbicides account for only 10 percent of the energy consumption of conventional corn production in the Rodale tests, and the pesticides even less than that. (Such chemicals are off-limits to organic farmers.) However, herbicide use may be on the rise on conventional farms, which would increase energy costs.

> **FAST FACT**
>
> The Organic Trade Association claims that organic farmers prevent water from being polluted by the nitrogen and chemicals used in conventional farming. Furthermore, the association says that organic farming methods build healthy soil that retains water, rather than wasting it.

Organic Foods Require Less Energy to Produce than Conventionally Grown Food

According to the Food and Agriculture Organization of the United Nations, in most cases, organic agriculture uses from 30 to 50 percent less energy in production than comparable conventional agriculture. It also typically uses energy more efficiently than nonorganic agriculture. A comparison of twelve different crops/foods found that most required less energy than their conventional counterparts.

Energy used to produce food products in organic agriculture systems compared to conventional systems

Food	Energy Used
Leeks	58% less
Milk	38% less
Beef	35% less
Wheat	29% less
Carrots	25% less
Lamb	20% less
Onions	16% less
Pig meat	13% less
Potatoes	2% more
Eggs	14% more
Tomatoes (long season)	30% more
Chicken	32% more

Taken from: Holly Hill. "Comparing Energy Use In Conventional and Organic Cropping Systems." ATTRA—National Sustainable Agriculture Information Service, 2009, p. 7.

"The conventional farmers at Rodale are beginning to see super-weeds that are resistant to Roundup," says Smallwood, referring to a popular weedkiller. "They now have to go back and apply a secondary herbicide."

Organic Saves Energy

A handful of larger meta-analyses, which combine the results of many different studies, have also found organic farms to be better energy misers than their conventional counterparts, and they put the organic advantage at closer to 20 percent per hectare. (In a couple of sectors, including poultry, conventional farming used slightly less energy than organic farming. Organically raised birds don't grow as quickly.)

It should be noted that farming accounts for only 35 percent of the energy embedded in your food, according to some estimates. The majority of the energy goes to transportation, cooking and the disposal of waste. Going organic can cut your energy consumption and greenhouse gas emissions, but other changes, such as more energy-efficient cooking methods, may have a greater impact.

The same caveat that applied to land use analysis also applies here. Environmental impact cannot be reduced to a single number such as productivity or energy consumption per acre.

EVALUATING THE AUTHOR'S ARGUMENTS:

In this viewpoint Brian Palmer makes his argument that organic farming conserves resources by examining its efficient use of energy. In the following viewpoint Agence France-Presse reports on a study examining the large amounts of land needed to yield high quantities of organic crops. After weighing the differences in energy and land use, at what conclusion do you arrive regarding organic farming's resource intensiveness?

Organic Farms' Need for More Land Is Bad for Earth: Study

"Many previous studies have shown large yields for organic farming but ignored the size of the area planted—which is often bigger than in conventional farming."

Agence France-Presse

The French news agency, Agence France-Presse (AFP), is the oldest and, alongside Associated Press and Reuters, one of the largest news agencies in the world. In the following viewpoint the author reports on a study that reviewed multiple studies for crop yields per unit area. The findings were that organic crops yielded up to one-third less than conventional farming. Critics of organic farming say that lower yields means more land must be used to equal the production of conventional farming. The study found conditions that favored conventional farming, such as irrigation, and practices that helped improve organic yield over time, such as crop rotation. Organic farmers argue that land use is just one aspect of organic farming, and critics should look at energy use, for example, which is less for organic than for conventional.

1. As stated by the author, what was the smallest percentage difference and what was the largest percentage difference between organic and conventional farming yields per unit area?
2. According to the viewpoint, what kinds of crops perform better in organic systems?
3. As stated in the article, what other aspect of organic farming besides energy use do supporters of organic farming use to counter the problem raised by land use?

PARIS—Organic farming may yield up to a third less of some crop types, according to a study proposing a hybrid with conventional agriculture as the best way to feed the world without destroying it.

Organic farming seeks to limit the use of chemical pesticides and fertilizers, but critics suggest lower crop yields require bigger swaths of land for the same output as conventional farms.

This would conceivably require parts of forests and other natural areas being turned into farmland, undoing some of the environmental gains of organic tilling methods, they say.

The new study by Canadian and American researchers, published in *Nature* Wednesday, reviewed 66 studies comparing the yields of 34 different crop species in organic and conventional farming systems. The review limited itself to studies assessing the total land area used, allowing researchers to compare crop yields per unit area. Many previous studies have shown large yields for organic farming but ignored the size of the area planted—which is often bigger than in conventional farming.

The analysis found that organic yields are as much as 34 percent lower for some crops than those from comparable conventional farming practices.

Particularly poor candidates for organic farming are vegetables and some cereal crops such as wheat, which make up much of the food consumed around the world.

Particularly good performers were fruit and oilseeds such as soybeans—yielding just 3% less, in ideal farming conditions, than conventionally grown crops that benefit from chemical pest killers and nutrients, the researchers found.

The findings contradict those of earlier studies that organic farming matched, or even exceeded, conventional yields.

"Today's organic systems may nearly rival conventional yields in some cases . . . but often they do not," said the report.

The study's lead author, Verena Seufert, an Earth system scientist at McGill University in Montreal, said the findings pointed to a mix of organic and conventional farming for the future.

"We identify, for example, legume crops and perennial crops as performing better in organic systems than annual and non-legume crops. We also see that organic systems do much better if the farmers apply good management practices," such as crop rotation and effective pest and nutrient control.

"We identify the situations where organic does well and we also identify the situations where it does not do so well, for example under irrigated conditions where the conventional yields can be just so high that organic agriculture can't match these yields."

A single system of "either organic or conventional is much too simplistic," said Ms Seufert.

"We should try to learn from those systems that perform well in terms of yield but also environmental performance and just adopt the systems in those places where they do well.

The study also found that organic yields rose over time as soil fertility and management skills improved.

Canada's organic farmers, more than 3,000 strong, rely on such techniques as crop rotation, green manure, compost and biological pest control. They exclude or severely limit the use of synthetic fertilizers, pesticides and animal hormones.

Beth McMahon, who heads the Canadian Organic Growers, said farmers are trying to find the best practices in both approaches.

> **FAST FACT**
>
> According to a 2012 study published in the journal *Nature*, because organic fields have lower yields than conventional fields, organic crops require more land and resources, which causes more deforestation, loss of species, and other environmental harms.

Organic Farming Requires Lots of Land

Studies show that per acre, organic crops yield less food than conventional crops. Opponents of organic farming argue that it wastes land. This chart shows many organic crops that have much lower yields, and thus require more land to grow the same amount of food.

Yields for Organic Vegetables Relative to Conventional Vegetables

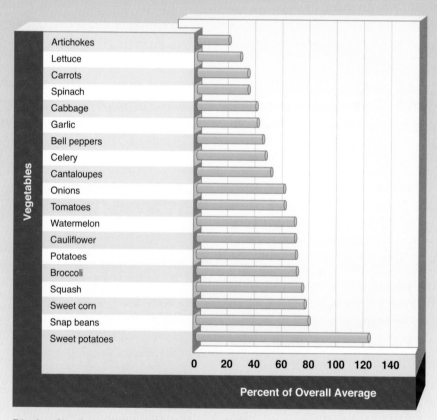

Taken from: Steve Savage. Appliedmythology.com, January 31, 2011.

"Oil-based fertilizers and conventional agriculture can be very expensive, for instance," she said. "When oil prices go up, fertilizer prices go up. A lot of farmers are looking to organic research to see what the alternatives are."

Ms McMahon said criticism of organic farming often misses the point.

"It's not just about land use," she said. "That's a very limited view of the benefits of organic agriculture."

She said organic farming uses far less energy than conventional farming, because energy isn't wasted producing and using pesticides and fertilizers.

Organic producer Burt Hodgins, who farms 600 acres near Kincardine, Ont., said his yields are lower than similarly sized conventional operations, but argues the benefits of organic farming outweigh that.

"Of course, if you use more acres, eventually you won't have enough acres," he said. "But if your chemical spray pollutes the drinking water, how is that related to whether you've used more acres or not? I don't see the difference whether you use 10 acres or eight acres to produce it."

Mr. Hodgins grows soybeans and certain types of wheat that the study identified as being the worst performers for organic farming.

But he said demand in Ontario and the European Union means his specialized organic produce always has buyers.

The present study considered only yield differences; Ms Seufert's next project is to analyse existing research on the environmental impacts of organic and conventional agriculture.

With files from Agence France-Presse, Nature *magazine and Peter Henderson for Postmedia News.*

EVALUATING THE AUTHOR'S ARGUMENTS:

The author, Agence France-Presse, reports on a study that finds organic farming may produce up to 34 percent less per unit area than conventional farming for certain crops but also brings up other factors that may mitigate those findings. Based on this and other viewpoints in this book, do you think organic farming on the whole wastes or conserves resources? Explain your answer.

Organic Crops Can Feed the World

Barry Estabrook

"Not only [can] organic . . . feed nine billion human beings but . . . it is the only hope we have of doing so."

Barry Estabrook is the author of the book *Tomatoland* and runs the website Politics of the Plate, which covers food and politics. In the following viewpoint he argues that organic farming techniques can produce enough food to feed the entire planet's population. He cites numerous studies that found organic farming techniques produced high crop yields with less water, energy, pesticides, and fertilizers than conventional crops. Organic farming techniques are so effective, in fact, that Estabrook says numerous studies recommend them as the way to alleviate hunger in places where famine and starvation are serious problems. Estabrook says people who characterize organic farming as too small scale to address world hunger are misinformed about organic farming's sustainability and effectiveness.

AS YOU READ, CONSIDER THE FOLLOWING QUESTIONS:

1. Who is Steve Kopperud, and how does he factor into the author's argument?

2. What did a 2008 study by the United Nations find about how using organic farming affected crop yields in twenty-four African countries?
3. How many papers does Estabrook say were published between 1999 and 2007 about whether organic food could feed the world? How many found it could not?

"We all have things that drive us crazy," wrote Steve Kopperud in a blog post this fall [2011] for Brownfield, an organization that disseminates agricultural news online and through radio broadcasts. Kopperud, who is a lobbyist for agribusiness interests in Washington, D.C., then got downright personal: "Firmly ensconced at the top of my list are people who consider themselves experts on an issue when judging by what they say and do, they're sitting high in an ivory tower somewhere contemplating only the 'wouldn't-it-be-nice' aspects."

At the top of that heap, Kopperud put Michael Pollan and Marion Nestle, a contributor to *Atlantic Life* and the author of *Food Politics*, the title of both her most well-known book and her daily blog.

"There's a huge chunk of reality missing from Dr. Nestle's academic approach to life," Kopperud wrote. "The missing bit is, quite simply, the answer to the following question: How do you feed seven billion people today and nine billion by 2040 through organic, natural, and local food production?" He then answers his own question. "You can't."

As a journalist who takes issues surrounding food production seriously, I too have things that drive me crazy.

At the top of my list are agribusiness advocates such as Kopperud (and, more recently, Steve Sexton of [the book] *Freakonomics*) who dismiss well-thought-out concerns about today's dysfunctional food production system with the old saw that organic farming can't save the world. They persist in repeating this as an irrefutable fact, even as one scientific study after another concludes the exact opposite: not only that organic can indeed feed nine billion human beings but that it is the only hope we have of doing so.

Pineapples grow on an organic farm in Togo in West Africa. A United Nations examination of farming in twenty-four African countries found that organic or near-organic farming resulted in yield increases of more than 100 percent.

Organic Techniques Improve Crop Yields

"There isn't enough land to feed the nine billion people" is one tired argument that gets trotted out by the anti-organic crowd, including Kopperud. That assertion ignores a 2007 study led by Ivette Perfecto, of the University of Michigan, showing that in developing countries, where the chances of famine are greatest, organic methods could double or triple crop yields.

"My hope is that we can finally put a nail in the coffin of the idea that you can't produce enough food through organic agriculture," Perfecto told Science Daily at the time.

Too bad solid, scientific research hasn't been enough to drive that nail home. A 2010 United Nations [U.N.] study concluded that organic and other sustainable farming methods that come under the umbrella of what the study's authors called "agroecology" would be necessary to feed the future world. Two years earlier, a U.N. examination of farming in 24 African countries found that organic or near-organic farming resulted in yield increases of more than 100 percent. Another U.N.-supported report entitled "Agriculture at a Crossroads", compiled by 400 international experts, said that the way the world grows food will have to change radically to meet future demand. It called for governments to pay more attention to small-scale farmers and sustainable practices—shooting down the bigger-is-inevitably-better notion that huge factory farms and their efficiencies of scale are necessary to feed the world.

Suspicious of the political motives of the U.N.? Well, there's a study that came out in 2010 from the all-American National Research Council. Written by professors from seven universities, including the University of California, Iowa State University,

> ## FAST FACT
>
> The 2010 United Nations report *Agroecology and the Right to Food* maintains that organic sustainable farming could double food production within ten years in countries where hunger is greatest.

and the University of Maryland, the report finds that organic farming, grass-fed livestock husbandry, and the production of meat and crops on the same farm will be needed to sustain food production in this country.

Organic Can Stave Off World Hunger

The Pennsylvania-based Rodale Institute is an unequivocal supporter of all things organic. But that's no reason to dismiss its 2008 report "The Organic Green Revolution", which provides a concise argument for why a return to organic principles is necessary to stave off world hunger, and which backs the assertion with citations of more than 50 scientific studies.

Rodale concludes that farming must move away from using unsustainable, increasingly unaffordable, petroleum-based fertilizers and pesticides and turn to "organic, regenerative farming systems that sustain and improve the health of the world population, our soil, and

Organic Crops Have High Yields

Long-term studies of corn and soybean crops have shown they can outproduce or produce about as much food as crops grown by conventional methods.

Average Yields (1998–2010)

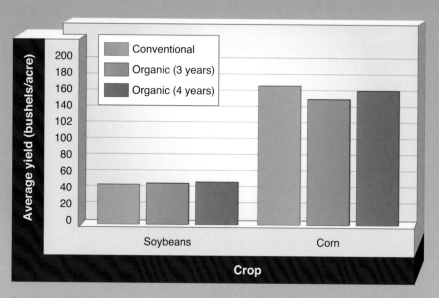

Taken from: Leopold Center for Sustainable Agriculture. Iowa State University. Long-Term Agroecological Research Experiment (LTAR), 2011.

our environment." The science the report so amply cites shows that such a system would

- give competitive yields to "conventional" methods
- improve soil and boost its capacity to hold water, particularly important during droughts
- save farmers money on pesticides and fertilizers
- save energy because organic production requires 20 to 50 percent less input
- mitigate global warming because cover crops and compost can sequester close to 40 percent of global CO_2 emissions
- increase food nutrient density

Organic Can Feed the World

What is notably lacking in the "conventional" versus organic debate are studies backing up the claim that organic can't feed the world's growing population. In an exhaustive review using Google and several academic search engines of all the scientific literature published between 1999 and 2007 addressing the question of whether or not organic agriculture could feed the world, the British Soil Association, which supports and certifies organic farms, found that there had been 98 papers published in the previous eight years addressing the question of whether organic could feed the world. Every one of the papers showed that organic farming had that potential. Not one argued otherwise.

The most troubling part of Kopperud's post is where he says that he finds the food movement of which Pollan and Nestle are respected leaders "almost dangerous." He's wrong. The real danger is when an untruth is repeated so often that people accept it as fact.

Given that the current food production system, which is really a 75-year-old experiment, leaves nearly one billion of the world's seven billion humans seriously undernourished today, the onus should be on the advocates of agribusiness to prove their model can feed a future population of nine billion—not the other way around.

EVALUATING THE AUTHOR'S ARGUMENTS:

Barry Estabrook quotes from several sources to support the points he makes in this viewpoint. Make a list of everyone he quotes, including their credentials and the nature of their comments. Then analyze how Estabrook uses these quotes—are they used to directly support his arguments? Or do they serve to point out the absurdity of a particular position? Explain whether you found the use of quotes in the viewpoint effective, and why.

Organic Crops Cannot Feed the World

James McWilliams

"Organic may not be 'the' solution to global food demand, but it can certainly be part of it."

Organic farming techniques do not produce enough food to reasonably feed the entire world, argues James McWilliams in the following viewpoint. He says organic food accounts for a miniscule amount of the total food grown in the United States. With the world's population growing and the need to produce even more food on even less land, McWilliams thinks it is unreasonable to think organic farming can meet this demand. Although certain kinds of organic crops have higher yields than their conventional counterparts, organic farming techniques typically yield significantly fewer staple crops that are critical to the food supply. McWilliams says it is these staple crops that must perform if the entire world is to benefit from organic agriculture. He predicts that organic farming will play only a small role in the solution to global food demand. McWilliams is the author of *Just Food: Where Locavores Get It Wrong and How We Can Truly Eat Responsibly*. He is an associate professor of history at Texas State University.

The Food and Agriculture Organization predicts that the global population will increase by 2.3 billion between now and 2050. This demographic explosion, intensified by an emerging middle class in China and India, will require the world's farmers to grow at least 70 percent more food than we now produce. Making matters worse, there's precious little arable land left for agricultural expansion. Barring a radical rejection of the Western diet, skyrocketing demand for food will have to be met by increasing production on pre-existing acreage. No matter how effectively we streamline access to existing food supplies, 90 percent of the additional calories required by mid-century will have to come through higher yields per acre.

How this will happen is one of the more contentious issues in agriculture. A particularly vocal group insists that we can avoid a 21st-century Malthusian crisis [forced return to subsistence farming] by transitioning wholesale to organic production—growing food without synthetic chemicals in accordance with the environmentally beneficial principles of agro-ecology. As recently as last September [2010] the Rodale Institute, an organization dedicated to the promotion of organic farming, reiterated this precept in no uncertain terms. "Organic farming," it declared, "is the only way to feed the world."

This is an exciting claim. Organic agriculture, after all, is the only approach to growing food that places primary emphasis on enhancing soil health. But is the assertion accurate? Can we actually feed the world with organic agriculture?

Organic Farms Produce a Modicum of Food

New research undertaken by Dr. Steve Savage, an agricultural scientist and plant pathologist, indicates that it's unlikely. In 2008 the USDA's [US Department of Agriculture's] National Agricultural Statistics

A crop of rapeseed (from which canola oil is made) awaits harvesting in Canada. According to a study cited by the author, canola was the only row-crop with greater yields when grown organically versus conventionally.

Service conducted the first comprehensive survey of certified organic agriculture. The study—which had a 90 percent participation rate among U.S. organic farmers who responded to the 2007 Census of Agriculture—recorded acreage, yield, and value for dozens of crops on more than 14,500 farms, in all 50 states.

Savage took these unprecedented USDA/NASS [National Agricultural Statistics Service] data and compared them with similar USDA statistics from conventional agriculture during the same crop year. (The USDA tallies conventional agriculture stats every year in order to track U.S. agricultural output over time.) The reason why the USDA did not make the comparison to organic production itself is anyone's guess. But what Savage found strongly suggests that organic production, for all its ecological benefits, is in no position to confront the world's impending demand for food.

Perhaps Savage's most striking finding is how few U.S. acres are actually in organic production. Characterizations of organic agriculture routinely portray it as a hard-charging underdog capable of competing for market share with conventional agribusiness. The USDA's Economic Research Service, for example, notes how "Organic agriculture has become one of the fastest growing segments of US agriculture." It's surprising, then, that the 1.6 million acres of harvested organic cropland in 2008 comprised a mere 0.52 percent of total crop acreage in the United States, as Savage found.

Savage's methodology couldn't have been simpler: He lined up and charted organic and conventional yield data for the same crop and state in which they were harvested. Although Savage was working with, as he put it, "the largest such data set on Organic that I have heard of," it wasn't without limitations. The USDA/NASS studies tracked harvested acres without differentiating between irrigated and non-irrigated acreage; it gathered data on planted vs. harvested acres for some crops but not others; it did not account for systems in which "baby vegetable" crops (usually organic) are grown in short rotations on the same plot (such as spinach, lettuce, and carrots) and thus have lower yields; and it omitted some data that would have revealed too much information about individual farmers, in cases where very few growers produce a particular crop.

Higher Yields of the Wrong Crops

But even with these qualifications, the numbers are discouraging for the organic option. The rubber really hits the road when it comes to yield. To its credit, organic does quite well in many cases: Sweet potatoes, raspberries, canola, and hay all yielded higher nationally than their conventional counterparts. At the state level, organic squash did better in Oregon than conventional squash; in Arizona and Colorado, organic apples yielded slightly higher than conventional ones; and in Washington state organic peaches beat out conventional varieties. In essence, there's a lot here for organic supporters to cherry-pick as evidence of organic's yield potential (but not cherries, which yielded much lower).

FAST FACT

In 2008 the US Department of Agriculture recorded that 2.5 million acres of cropland in the United States were certified as organic, constituting only 0.7 percent of the total 370 million acres of US cropland.

Unfortunately, there's little hope in feeding the world with higher yields of sweet potatoes, peaches, and raspberries—much less hay. What matters most is the performance of basic row-crops. As it turns

Organic Crops Underperform

Studies have shown that organic yields of edible crops and staples are much lower than those grown by conventional methods. Organic apple yields, for example, are typically lower than conventionally grown apples. Yields of garlic, broccoli, snap beans, spinach, carrots, and numerous other crops are lower too.

Apple Yields for Major States

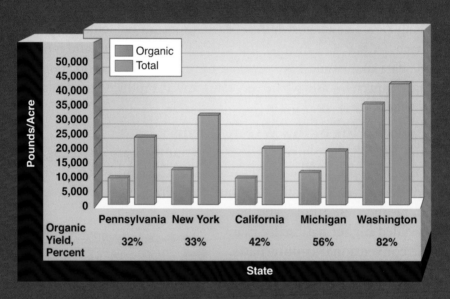

Taken from: Steve Savage. Appliedmythology.com, January 31, 2011.

out, yields were dramatically lower for these commodities: 40 percent lower for winter wheat, 29 percent lower for corn, 34 percent lower for soy, 53 percent lower for spring wheat, 41 percent lower for rice, 58 percent lower for sorghum, and 64 percent lower for millet. Canola was the only row-crop with greater yields with organic farming.

What we might call "secondary staples" did poorly as well. The organic option yielded 28 percent lower for potatoes, 21 percent lower for sweet corn, 38 percent lower for onions, 19 percent lower for snap beans, and 52 percent lower for bell peppers. Perhaps most distressingly, some of the healthiest foods on the planet yielded comparatively poorly under organic production: 42 percent lower for blueberries, 23 percent lower for broccoli, and almost 40 percent lower for tomatoes.

Too Small to Be the Only Solution

Given these figures, a switch to organic agriculture would require a 43 percent increase over current U.S. cropland, according to Savage. As he puts it, "On a land-area basis, this additional area would be 97% the physical size of Spain or 71% the size of Texas." (Yes, Texas is bigger than Spain.) These are depressing figures, especially in light of the fact that global food demand is entering a 40-year upward trend. It's no wonder that Savage, who spent part of his career developing organic pest controls, concludes that organic "is too small and unproductive to ever be the 'solution' to our need to simultaneously feed the world and protect the environment," as he told me via e-mail.

So should we dismiss organic agriculture outright? Absolutely not. Organic may not be "the" solution to global food demand, but it can certainly be part of it. As Jason Clay, senior vice president of the World Wildlife Fund, writes, "I think we need a new kind of agriculture—kind of third agriculture, between the big agribusiness, commercial approach to agriculture research, there's every reason to hope that organic yields will improve and that the organic model will become more prominent. The fact that we're not yet there, as Savage's study verifies, doesn't mean we should abandon the quest for agricultural systems that are both high yielding and as ecologically responsible as they can be.

EVALUATING THE AUTHOR'S ARGUMENTS:

James McWilliams (author of this viewpoint) and Barry Estabrook (author of the previous viewpoint) disagree with each other over whether organic farming techniques can produce enough food to feed the entire world. After reading both viewpoints, with which author do you agree, and why? Discuss which piece of evidence swayed you— it could be the identity of the author, a fact or opinion expressed in his viewpoint, or another piece of evidence.

Chapter 3

What Is the Nature of Organic Food?

In 2010, according to the Organic Trade Association, organic food and drink sales totaled $26.7 billion in the United States.

Organic Food Is Elitist

Roger Cohen

"Organic has long since become an ideology, the romantic back-to-nature obsession of an upper middle class able to afford it."

Organic food is overpriced and classist, argues Roger Cohen in the following viewpoint. He says organic foods are no more nutritious or healthy than conventionally grown foods, so there is no reason for customers to pay so much money for them. Organic farming techniques are unable to produce enough food to feed the world's population, so Cohen views them as feel-good products that benefit the rich only. He thinks of organic food as something upper-middle-class people buy to project a certain image about themselves, just as they might buy expensive clothes or an overpriced car. For most people, says Cohen, organic food offers nothing. He says people should view organic food as something that is only good for making wealthy, pampered people feel better about themselves. Cohen is a columnist for the *New York Times*, where this viewpoint was originally published.

AS YOU READ, CONSIDER THE FOLLOWING QUESTIONS:

1. How much did organic food and drink sales total in the United States in 2010, according to Cohen?
2. To what does Cohen compare buying organic baby food?
3. What were the findings of a 2012 study by Stanford researchers, according to Cohen?

At some point—perhaps it was gazing at a Le Pain Quotidien menu offering an "organic baker's basket served with organic butter, organic jam and organic spread" as well as seasonally organic orange juice—I found I just could not stomach the "O" word or what it stood for any longer.

A Class-Driven Decision

Organic has long since become an ideology, the romantic back-to-nature obsession of an upper middle class able to afford it and oblivious, in their affluent narcissism, to the challenge of feeding a planet whose population will surge to 9 billion before the middle of the century and whose poor will get a lot more nutrients from the two regular carrots they can buy for the price of one organic carrot.

An effective form of premium branding rather than a science, a slogan rather than better nutrition, "organic" has oozed over the menus, markets and malls of the world's upscale neighborhood at a remarkable pace. In 2010, according to the Organic Trade Association, organic food and drink sales totaled $26.7 billion in the United States, or about 4 percent of the overall market, having grown steadily since 2000. The British organic market is also large; menus like to mention that bacon comes from pampered pigs at the Happy Hog farm down the road.

In the midst of the fad few questions have been asked. But the fact is that buying organic baby food, a growing sector, is like paying to send your child to private school: It is a class-driven decision that demonstrates how much you love your offspring but whose overall impact on society is debatable.

Organic, Schmorganic

So I cheered this week [in September 2012] when Stanford University concluded, after examining four decades of research, that fruits and

After examining four decades of research, Stanford University scientists concluded that fruits and vegetables labeled organic are, on average, no more nutritious than their cheaper conventional counterparts.

vegetables labeled organic are, on average, no more nutritious than their cheaper conventional counterparts. The study also found that organic meats offered no obvious health advantages. And it found that organic food was not less likely to be contaminated by dangerous bacteria like E.coli.

The takeaway from the study could be summed up in two words: Organic, schmorganic. That's been my feeling for a while.

Now let me say three nice things about the organic phenomenon. The first is that it reflects a growing awareness about diet that has spurred quality, small-scale local farming that had been at risk of disappearance.

The second is that even if it's not better for you, organic farming is probably better for the environment because less soil, flora and fauna

"You may not feel any healthier right away, but you'll definitely feel more smug."

are contaminated by chemicals (although of course, without fertilizers, you have to use more land to grow the same amount of produce or feed the same amount of livestock.) So this is food that is better ecologically even if it is not better nutritionally.

The third is that the word organic—unlike other feel-good descriptions of food like "natural"—actually means something. Certification procedures in both the United States and Britain are strict. In the United States, organic food must meet standards ensuring that genetic engineering, synthetic fertilizers, sewage and irradiation were not used in the food's production. It must also be produced using methods that, according to the Department of Agriculture, "foster cycling of resources, promote ecological balance and conserve biodiversity."

Still, the organic ideology is an elitist, pseudoscientific indulgence shot through with hype. There is a niche for it, if you can afford to shop at Whole Foods [natural foods supermarket], but the future is nonorganic.

We Need to Get Serious About the World's Needs

To feed a planet of 9 billion people, we are going to need high yields not low yields; we are going to need genetically modified crops; we are going to need pesticides and fertilizers and other elements of the industrialized food processes that have led mankind to be better fed and live longer than at any time in history.

Logically, the organic movement should favor genetically modified produce. If you cannot use pesticides or fertilizers, you might at least want to modify your crops so they are more resilient and plentiful. But that would go against the ideology and romance of a movement that says: We are for nature, everyone else is against nature.

I'd rather be against nature and have more people better fed. I'd rather be serious about the world's needs. And I trust the monitoring agencies that ensure pesticides are used at safe levels—a trust the Stanford study found to be justified.

Nothing More than a Romantic Fable

Martin Orbach, the co-founder and program director of the Abergavenny Food Festival in Britain, owns a company called Shepherds that produces a superb sheep's milk ice-cream sold at a store in Hay-on-Wye. It has a cult following at the Hay literary festival and beyond. Journalists, Orbach told me, regularly report that they have eaten an "organic sheep's milk ice cream."

The only catch is this is not true. "We have never said it's organic because it would be illegal for us to do so," Orbach said. "But it fits with the story of a small sheep's milk ice-cream maker."

Organic is a fable of the pampered parts of the planet—romantic and comforting. Now, thanks to Stanford researchers, we know just how replete with myth the "O" fable is.

Organic Food Is Not Elitist

Joel Salatin

Organic food is not elitist, argues Joel Salatin in the following viewpoint. He says it is natural for high-quality goods to cost more than their lower-quality counterparts. People are willing to pay more for finely made clothing and indulgent vacations, so to him it makes sense that they would also be willing to pay a premium for food that is healthier, better tasting, safer, more nutritious, and better grown than conventional food. Salatin says that organic foods cost much less than preprocessed foods and far less than unhealthy products like alcohol and tobacco. He says that if the true environmental and production costs of conventional foods were more obvious, organic foods would seem much less expensive in comparison. He concludes there is nothing elitist about choosing healthy, sustainably farmed, environmentally responsible food whose cost reflects its quality. Salatin runs Polyface Farms in Virginia, an organic farm enterprise.

"The charge of elitism is both unfair and silly."

Because high-quality local food often carries a higher price tag than food generated by the industrial system, the charge of elitism coming from industrial foodists is often vitriolic, and embarrassed foodies agonize over the label. For all their positive energy surrounding food, I've found latent guilt among this group—guilt for paying more for local food when others are starving, guilt for caring about taste when others would happily eat anything. Instead of cowering in self-guilt, let's confront the issue of prices head on.

Organic Food Has Real Value

First, it's better food. It tastes better. It handles better. And it's safer: Anyone buying chemicalized, drug-infused food is engaging in risky behavior.

It's also nutritionally superior. For those willing to see, scientific data shows fresh foods' conjugated linoleic acid, vitamins, minerals, brix readings, omega 3–omega 6 ratios, and polyunsaturated fat profiles are empirically superior.

Better stuff is worth more.

Second, economies of scale will continue to progress as more people patronize local food, which will bring prices down. The collaborative aggregation and distribution networks that have been fine-tuned by mega-food companies can and will be duplicated locally as volume increases and regional food systems get more creative.

Third, eating unprocessed foods is the best way to bring down your grocery bill, regardless of where the food originated. A 10-pound bag of potatoes costs the same as a 1-pound bag of potato chips. Cultivating domestic culinary arts and actually reinhabiting our kitchens—which we've remodeled and gadgetized at great cost—can wean all of us away from expensive processed food. A whole pound of our farm's grass-finished ground beef, which can feed four adults, costs about the same as a Happy Meal. (And guess which one is more healthful?)

The Truth About Food Costs

Fourth, non-scalable government regulations—which are designed to protect eaters from the dangers inherent in the industrial food complex but are not relevant in a transparent, regional food system—inordinately discriminate against smaller processing businesses like abattoirs, kitchens, and canneries, because the costs of complying with the (inappropriate) paperwork and infrastructure requirements cannot be spread out over a large volume of product. These regulations lead to price prejudice at the community-based scale: Small processors are at a disadvantage because they must pass those costs on to consumers, making their products more expensive than the mass-produced ones. These burdensome regulations also discourage entrepreneurs from entering local food commerce.

Fifth, unlike huge, single-crop or single-animal farms, diversified farms like ours do not receive government subsidies. Nor do the production, processing, and marketing of our food create collateral damage like that caused by factory farming—damage left for taxpayers to fix. Subsidies and government clean-up measures are not

> **FAST FACT**
>
> According to the International Society for Ecology and Culture, government subsidies for conventional foods make them artificially cheap and make consumers think local organic foods have "elitist" prices. 7-Eleven's frozen Slurpee drinks are only cheaper than juice, it says, because corn sweetener, a main ingredient, is subsidized.

included in the price you pay for processed food at the grocery store, but if they were, local food would not seem so expensive in comparison.

Consider the Rhode Island–sized area in the Gulf of Mexico now known as a "dead zone" because nothing can survive in the oxygen-starved water, a result of manure and pesticide runoff. Who pays for the clean up and the reversal efforts? Who pays to address antibiotic-resistant strains of bacteria like MRSA [methicillin-resistant *Staphylococcus aureus*], caused by the overuse of antibiotics in CAFOs (concentrated animal feeding operations)? Who pays to treat people with Type II diabetes, which they get from consuming processed food that is sold cheaply because the corporations making it have received subsidies? Who pays to clean up stinky rural neighborhoods with densely populated poultry and livestock compounds? And what is the value of the land irreversibly damaged by bad farming practices?

Everyone Has Indulgences

Sixth—and this is where I wanted to head with this discussion—plenty of money already exists in our economic system to pay for good food. Can you think of anything people buy that they don't need? Tobacco products, $100 designer jeans with holes already in the knees, KFC, soft drinks made with high fructose corn syrup, Disney vacations, large-screen TVs, jarred baby food? America spends more on veterinary care for pets than the entire continent of Africa spends on medical care for humans.

I won't belabor the point, but if you took all the money people spend on unnecessary baubles and junk food, it would be enough for everyone to eat like kings. We could all be elitists.

With that money, we could create a suburb of Lake Wobegon [fictional Midwestern town], where all the people eat food that is above average. Almost everyone I know who owns a community supported agriculture (CSA) share could afford to purchase an extra one for an impoverished family. And if you had to give up a few $4 lattes to do it? What a pity.

High-Quality Food Should Cost More

This winter [2010], the Front Range Permaculture Institute invited me to come to Fort Collins, Colorado, and give a speech at a fundraising event. They filled a huge community theater with people, and ticket sales were enough to pay my travel and honorarium—with enough left over to buy 40 CSA shares for poor families in their community. What a wonderfully empowering local effort. (They didn't wait for a government program.) Perhaps nothing would reduce perceptions of elitism faster than foodies buying CSA shares for impoverished families.

At the risk of sounding uncharitable, I think we need to quit being victims and bring about change ourselves. Don't complain

Joel Salatin (pictured) runs the organic Polyface Farms in Virginia. He says it is natural for high-quality goods to cost more than their lower-quality counterparts. To him it makes sense that people would be willing to pay a premium for food that is healthier, tastes better, is safer and more nutritious, and is grown with more care than conventional food.

about being unable to afford high-quality local food when your grocery cart is full of beer, cigarettes, and *People* magazine. Most people are more connected to the celebrities in *People* than the food that will become flesh of their flesh and bone of their bones at the next meal.

Organic Food Has Value

According to a 2013 report released by *Natural Foods Merchandiser,* sales of organic foods increased by 11 percent between 2011 and 2012. The report also found that about eight out of every ten parents buy organic at least some of the time.

Natural and conventional channels	2011 (in billions)	2012 (in billions)	Percent change
Meat, fish, poultry	$0.7	$0.8	13
Condiments	$0.8	$0.9	16
Snack foods	$1.2	$1.3	15
Breads and grains	$2.5	$2.7	8
Beverages	$2.8	$3.1	10
Packaged/prepared foods	$2.9	$3.2	10
Dairy	$4.1	$4.4	7
Fruits and vegetables	$8.8	$9.9	13
Total	**$23.8**	**$26.3**	**11**

Taken from: *Natural Foods Merchandiser. 2013 Market Overview,* July 2013.

The other day I saw precooked bacon in a box at the supermarket—for $30 a pound. Do we really have to buy precooked bacon? If you took the average shopping cart in the checkout line and tossed out all the processed food—everything with an ingredient you can't pronounce, everything you can't re-create in your kitchen, and everything that won't rot—and substituted instead locally sourced, fresh items, you would be dollars ahead and immensely healthier.

We can all do better. If we can find money for movies, ski trips, and recreational cruises, surely we can find the money to purchase integrity food. The fact is that most of us scrounge together enough pennies to fund the passion of our hearts. If we would cultivate a passion for food like the one we've cultivated for clothes, cars, and entertainment, perhaps we would ultimately live healthier, happier lives.

Guilt-Free Organic Eating

To suggest that advocating for such a change makes me an elitist is to disparage positive decision making and behavior. Indeed, if that's elitism, I want it. The victim mentality our culture encourages actually induces guilt among people making progress. That's crazy. We should applaud positive behavior and encourage others to follow suit, not demonize and discourage it. Would it be better to applaud people who buy amalgamated, reconstituted, fumigated, irradiated, genetically modified industrial garbage?

The charge of elitism is both unfair and silly. We foodies are cultural change agents, positive innovators, integrity seekers. So hold your head high and don't apologize for making noble decisions.

EVALUATING THE AUTHOR'S ARGUMENTS:

In this viewpoint Joel Salatin uses facts, statistics, examples, and reasoning to make his argument that organic food is not elitist. He does not, however, use any quotations to support his point. If you were to rewrite this article and insert quotations, what authorities might you quote from? Where would you place the quotations, and why?

The Low-Down on Organic Foods

"*Also banned are ionizing radiation and various methods used to modify organisms . . . in ways that cannot be achieved under natural conditions.*"

Zak Solomon

Zak Solomon works with FoodSentry .org, an organization that works to protect American consumers from serious food-borne illness. Solomon is also a contributor to Food Safety News. In the following viewpoint Solomon reports on the requirements for organic foods. Organic foods must not be made with synthetic or other prohibited substances. Organic producers must be certified by an accredited certification agent, and products must be labeled according to what percentage of organically grown product they contain.

AS YOU READ, CONSIDER THE FOLLOWING QUESTIONS:

1. As stated by the author, what legislation governs the production of organic foods and what agency or organization enforces this legislation?
2. According to the viewpoint, what is one substance organic food must not come in contact with during production?
3. As stated in the article, what two tasks do certifying agents perform annually on organic producer operations?

This article is part one of three in a series on organic foods published by Food Sentry. This entry was originally published on Feb. 6, 2013.

Over the past decade, it's apparent that a lot of the country, if not the world, has been making a push toward a future where organic food products dominate the marketplace. The general consensus seems to be that organic food products are somehow better and safer than non-organic products. But why? What drives this consensus? Is it true? Is it as simple as "organic is better"?

Perhaps. But, as with many things, this kind of statement may be an all-too-common over-simplification of a more complicated topic. If only it were that simple. As Food Sentry analysts, we are naturally skeptical and curious and like to look deeper into the situation before making a judgment. Let's dive in and take a look at "organic" and see what the facts tell us.

What often seems to be lacking in the dialogue regarding organics is the knowledge of exactly what organic food products are. Most people have a notion of what it means but may not have all the details. In this first part of our three-part "Organic Foods" series, we'll be giving you the low-down on what it generally means for a product to be identified as "organic" in the U.S., and we'll provide you with more advanced knowledge that will help you to better judge organics on the whole.

FAST FACT

The US Department of Agriculture Organic seal on a package certifies that at least 95 percent—and up to 100 percent—of its content is organic. Companies that break the department's rules for organics may be fined eleven thousand dollars per violation.

To start things off, you should know that the organic market in the U.S. is regulated and governed under a piece of legislation called the "National Organics Program" (NOP) which is enforced and overseen by the United States Department of Agriculture (USDA), not the U.S. Food and Drug Administration (FDA). Within the NOP there are both general and specific guidelines that must be met by producers, including but not limited to: ingredient; contact substance and modification method specifications; product production, handling, and certification standards; and strict labeling requirements.

Ingredients, Contact Substances, and Modification Methods

In general, all agricultural products that are sold, labeled or represented as "organic" in any way must not have come in contact with sewage sludge during production and must be produced without the use of:

- synthetic substances,
- National Organic Program–prohibited non-synthetic substances,
- non-organic/non-agricultural and non-organic/agricultural substances used in or on processed products.

Also banned are ionizing radiation and various methods used to modify organisms and/or their growth and development in ways that cannot be achieved under natural conditions.

Although these rules apply to most substances in most situations, there are exceptions. A number of these types of substances and methods are actually permitted (typically in specific forms) for use in various applications specified within the NOP. A long list of these exceptions can be found here: Substance methods lists.

Product Production, Handling Requirements, and Certification

To produce and market organic products in the U.S., an organization must become certified by a USDA-accredited organics certification agent. In order to meet the USDA-established certification standards, producers and handlers must adhere to strict production guidelines that are specified further based on the product type, e.g., animal-based or plant-based.

Additionally, certification requires that producers and handlers employ stringent pest-management practices at their facilities and that they take all necessary measures to prevent the commingling of "organic" products with "non-organic" products and prohibited substances. Organics producers and handlers are required to keep detailed logs of almost every aspect of their operations, which are reviewed annually by certifying agents, who also perform annual on-site inspections.

Important!

For those readers who purchase organic products from farmers markets or other smaller food-selling operations, you may be interested to know that if the entity/individual you purchase from reports less than $5,000 annually from sales of organic products, they are not subject to the certification/verification as described above.

Labeling Requirements

In our opinion, food labeling in the U.S. is probably one of the most confusing, dysfunctional and often-misleading aspects of the food market. In fact, there is a whole industry devoted to helping manufacturers learn and apply labeling regulations. Unfortunately, "organic" product labeling is no exception, although at least use of the term "organic" is better regulated than the term "natural." What many people don't realize is that under the NOP, there are actually four different types of labels which classify organic products:

- "100 percent organic"
- "Organic"
- "Made with organic (specified ingredients or food groups)"
- "<70 percent organic"

Each of these labels represents certain specifications and product requirements, which are as follows:

- "100 percent organic" means: a raw or processed product that contains 100-percent organically produced ingredients (by weight or volume, excluding water or salt) that has been produced in accordance with the relevant production and handling guidelines set forth in the NOP. This product will have the words "100 percent organic" on the packaging, as well as the USDA seal and name and/or logo of the certifying agent.
- "Organic" means: a raw or processed product that contains at least 95-percent organically produced ingredients (by weight or volume, excluding water or salt) that has been produced in accordance with the guidelines set forth in the NOP. All other product ingredients must be produced organically (unless the ingredient isn't commercially available in organic form) or they must be non-agricultural substances or non-organically produced agricultural products produced in accordance with the relevant production and handling guidelines within the NOP. This product will have the word "Organic" on the packaging, as well as the USDA seal and name and/or logo of the certifying agent. Additionally, the

Organic Labeling Guidelines

Only products that meet specific criteria may display official organic seals.

Organic and use label	Use excluded methods	Use sewage sludge	Use ionizing radiation	Use substances not on national list	Contains added sulfites, nitrates, nitrites	Use nonorganic ingredients and label "when available"	Use both organic and nonorganic forms of same ingredient
"100 percent organic" Single/multiple ingredients completely organic	No	No	No	No	No	No	No
"Organic" Organic ingredients (95% or more)	No	No	No	No	No	No	No
Nonorganic ingredients (5% or more)	No	No	No	No	No	No	No
"Made with organic ingredients" Organic ingredients (70–95%)	No	No	No	No	No— except wine	No	No
Nonorganic ingredients (30% or less)	No	No	No	OK	OK	Not Applicable	Not Applicable
Less than 70% organic ingredients Organic ingredients (30% or less)	No	No	No	No	No— except wine	No	No
Nonorganic ingredients (70% or more)	OK	OK	OK	OK	OK	Not Applicable	Not Applicable

Taken from: United States Department of Agriculture, 2013.

packaging must display the percentage of organic ingredients in the product, and each individual ingredient that is organic in these products must be labeled as "organic" in the ingredients section of the packaging.

- "Made with organic (specified ingredients or food groups)" means: a multi-ingredient agricultural product that contains at least 70-percent organically produced ingredients (by weight or volume, excluding water or salt) that has been produced in accordance with the guidelines set forth in the NOP. This product will display the words "Made with organic" followed by three or fewer ingredients or food groups, as well as the total percentage of organic ingredients in the product and the name and logo of the certifying agent. Additionally, the individual ingredients that are organic in these products must be labeled as "organic" in the ingredients section of the packaging. These packages will not display the USDA seal.

- "<70 percent organic" means: a multi-ingredient agricultural product containing fewer than 70-percent organically produced ingredients (by weight or volume, excluding water or salt) that has been produced in accordance with the guidelines set forth in the NOP. Non-organic ingredients in these products are not subject to the requirements of the NOP. This product will only display the word "organic" next to organically produced ingredients in the ingredient statement on the packaging and the total percentage of organic ingredients in the product. These products will not display the USDA seal or any certifying agent's information.

The Low-Down

So there it is—the gist of what it means to be an organic product in the U.S. Your (hopefully) new and/or improved knowledge should serve you well as you navigate local groceries, co-ops and farmers markets. Unfortunately, however, the puzzle of organics is still incomplete since a question lingers: what are the actual differences between "organic" and "non-organic" products?

EVALUATING THE AUTHOR'S ARGUMENTS:

The author, Zak Solomon, reports on the requirements organic food producers must meet. How do you think the author of the following viewpoint, Mischa Popoff, would assess the stringency of these requirements? Which viewpoint do you agree with more? Why?

Viewpoint 4

Organic Labeling Is Not Based on Strict Requirements

Mischa Popoff

> *"The 'organic' label doesn't necessarily give you what you think you are buying."*

In the following viewpoint Mischa Popoff argues that an organic label does not mean what consumers think it does. He argues that to get an organic label, food manufacturers need not prove their product is organic or even necessarily submit it for testing; all they need to do is comply with paperwork and pay fees, and they will be granted the organic label. Popoff says that federally regulated, for-profit agencies sell the privilege of bearing an organic label to businesses that do not necessarily deserve it but can pay the money. To him this means the organic labeling system is nothing more than a scheme whereby the government and food producers make money off consumers who buy organic because they think they are doing something good for themselves. In reality, Popoff concludes, there is nothing beneficial about organic food or the labeling process. Popoff is a research associate at the Frontier Centre for Public Policy and the coauthor of the book *Canada's Organic Nightmare*.

As the holidays approach, Canadians are spending more time purchasing and preparing foodstuffs for their family tables. They're also looking for appealing, tasty, nutritious goods that will not upset their budgets.

Be prepared for the seasonal, united organic-food-movement appeal, calling on Canadians to buy certified-organic turkey, organic vegetables and fruit, organic breads and pastries, organic milk and meats, organic nuts, and even organic booze.

But is organic food purer, tastier and more nutritious?

An Honor System That Is Heavily Abused

A recent in-depth report on the Canadian organic sector published by The Frontier Centre points out that there is no systematic, empirical proof that food certified as organic is purer, tastier or more nutritious.

It turns out that a bevy of federally regulated, for-profit, organic certifying agencies sell the privilege to organic farmers, brokers, traders and processors to label their products "certified organic" in Canada.

And with the Canadian Food Inspection Agency's (CFIA) logo affixed to their products, premiums of 100 to 200 per cent are then garnered without a single test being performed.

It's all just a glorified, bureaucratic, tax-subsidized, public-private, abused honour system.

A Politicized Privilege

The politicized privilege to be deemed "certified-organic" in Canada is available to anyone, whether here in Canada or anywhere in the world. To qualify, just pay fees and fill out paperwork, even if you're in China, Mexico or Argentina. The honesty of the applicants is not verified. When staff at the CFIA finally carried out some secret tests on organic products, they were so taken aback by the results that they actually tried to suppress them.

There was a time when the CFIA considered organic testing. Testing is, after all, how the regular food system is kept safe. But the idea of applying science to the organic industry in Canada was dead-on-arrival thanks to the organic lobby; in spite of the fact that the cost of testing is one tenth that of the current paper-based system of record-checking.

No Testing, Just Paperwork

By relying exclusively on paperwork, Canada's for-profit organic certifiers benefit from highly lucrative revenues which, in turn, provide donations to activist organic groups which may explain their opposition to testing in spite of support for the idea from rank-and-file Canadian organic farmers.

In addition to up-front application and inspection fees, organic farmers and processors operating under CFIA "rules" are forced to pay royalties to their private certifiers between one and three per cent on their gross revenue from each and every transaction. It is akin to the franchise fees that fast-food restaurant owners pay to their head offices, with the difference that Canadian organic farmers and processors are paying for the use of the CFIA's logo on their finished products, not the private certifier's. And yet, the CFIA requires no testing. None.

As every lifestyle section in newspapers across the land pays homage to the certified-organic turkey and all the fixings (never asking whether it's worth it or whether it even helps a single Canadian farmer), remember that private organic certifiers only enforce the administrative rules of organic production in this country. While independent inspectors make pre-announced

> **FAST FACT**
>
> In 2012 the Centers for Disease Control and Prevention reported that thirty-three people in five states grew ill from eating a salad blend that had been certified organic but was contaminated with *E. coli.* Of the thirteen people hospitalized, two developed kidney failure.

A bottle of organic chardonnay is shown. The author says that none of the alleged mystical attributes of organic barley for beer or organic grapes for wine even has a chance of surviving the fermentation process.

visits once a year to each farm and facility, they don't do any testing. They only fill out paperwork.

In addition to organic foods, you'll also be hit with the idea of bringing in the New Year with certified-organic booze. Such claims could not possibly get any more absurd. None of the alleged mystical attributes of organic barley or grapes even has a chance of surviving the fermentation and distillation processes. So save your money.

The Organic Label Is Not Worth Much

Whether you're someone who only "goes organic" during festive occasions, or one of the millions of Canadians who buys organic food on a regular basis believing it's purer, more nutritious and more sustainable than regular food, let the buyer beware. The "organic" label doesn't necessarily give you what you think you are buying.

If you really want to help Canadian organic farmers, buy directly from them as you're not likely going to find their products on grocery-store shelves this Christmas season.

Otherwise, you may want to save the money for the children's toys instead.

> **EVALUATING THE AUTHOR'S ARGUMENTS:**
>
> In this viewpoint Mischa Popoff describes an organic labeling system that is corrupted by profit and bureaucracy. If you were to redesign the system, what would it look like? What would companies have to do to receive an organic label? What requirements or steps would there be? Describe five or six requirements that would constitute an organic labeling system you think would be free of corruption and would offer consumers a truly organic product.

Facts About Organic Food and Farming

Editor's note: These facts can be used in reports to add credibility when making important points or claims.

The Organic Foods Production Act of 1990 was passed in order to

- regulate organic foods on a national level,
- set clear standards for organic food labeling,
- protect consumers from foods that are mislabeled as organic,
- educate consumers and growers about what organic means,
- encourage interstate transport of organic foods,
- allow states to set even stricter rules than the federal government's, and
- authorize the formation of the National Organic Program and National Organic Standards Board.

According to the Organic Farming Research Foundation:

- Foods certified as organic are minimally processed, without artificial ingredients or preservatives.
- Organic foods must not contain synthetic chemicals, irradiation, or genetically modified ingredients.
- Certified organic farms are inspected regularly to ensure they have:
    - an organic system plan that describes how they produce their foods.
    - detailed records tracing all foods from the field to market.
    - buffer zones to prevent contamination by chemicals from neighboring farms.
    - proper methods of cleaning, pest control, storing ingredients, and transportation.
- About 2 percent of the food supply in the United States is certified organic.
- Organic fields yield 95 percent as much as—and have the potential to surpass—conventional crop fields.

- When farmers switch from conventional to organic growing, they usually experience a three-year period in which yields initially decrease but then bounce back.
- In 2007 the United States had about thirteen thousand certified organic producers, up from twenty-five hundred to three thousand in 1994.
- The US organic industry has increased by about 20 percent per year for more than ten years.

Since 2006 the US Department of Agriculture (USDA) has allowed thirty-eight nonorganic ingredients to be used in foods certified as organic. These include food colorings, hops, fish oils, and gelatin.

Opinions About Organic Food

According to a 2011 NPR-Thomson Reuters Health Poll:

- Fifty-eight percent of people prefer organic food over conventional food.
- Thirty-one percent favor conventional food over organics.
- Eleven percent have no preference.
- Fewer people age sixty-five and older prefer organics: 45 percent choose organics, 38 percent prefer conventional foods, and 17 percent have no preference.
- Thirty-four percent of people said that when at a restaurant, they choose dishes labeled as organic on the menu.
- Among people who prefer organic foods, 36 percent say it is because they want to support local farmers, while 34 percent say they wish to avoid toxins in conventional crops.

According to the Yale Rudd Center's 2009 report *Public Perceptions of Food Marketing to Youth*:

- Sixty-four percent of parents said the biggest barrier to ensuring that their children develop healthy eating habits is the cost of nutritious food.
- Fifty percent of parents named the cost of organic food as an obstacle to their kids' eating healthfully.
- Fifty-three percent of parents with a lower household income (less than forty thousand dollars) identified the cost of organic food as a

barrier to their children's healthy eating, compared to 38 percent of those with a higher income (more than seventy-five thousand dollars).

- Communities and the government need to address income disparity so that all children can have access to nutritious food.

Facts About Organic Food Safety

A 2009 study that the London School of Hygiene & Tropical Medicine conducted for the UK Food Standards Agency reviewed more than fifty thousand studies that compared nutritional content of organic and nonorganic foods (but ignored contaminants from pesticides). The researchers found:

- no differences between organic and conventional foods in ten of thirteen nutrients examined,
- nonorganic crops contained significantly more nitrogen,
- organic crops were significantly higher in phosphorus, and
- the differences were most likely from different fertilizers used and ripeness at harvest. Eating organic foods with nutrients at these levels is unlikely to provide any health benefit.

According to the Organic Center's report, *Nutritional Superiority of Organic Foods*:

- Scientists formed 236 pairs of foods, one organic and one conventional. They compared each pair's levels of eleven nutrients, which included:
  - four antioxidants,
  - vitamins A, C, and E,
  - two minerals—potassium and phosphorous,
  - nitrates (higher levels are less healthy), and
  - protein.
- In 145 pairs, or 61 percent of cases, the organic foods were more nutritional.
- Conventional foods had more nutrients in 37 percent of cases.
- There was no difference in 2 percent of cases.
- The organic foods had more antioxidants in about three-quarters of the pairs.

- One-quarter of the organic foods that were more nutritional were significantly so—at least 31 percent higher in nutrients than the conventional food.
- On average, the organic foods were 25 percent higher in nutrients.

According to the Organic Farming Research Foundation:

- A 2002 study found that 13 percent of organic produce samples contained insecticide residues, whereas 71 percent of conventional produce samples did.
- It is a misconception that organic foods have greater risk of *E. coli* because they are grown using raw manure. Conventional farmers use raw manure, too, with no regulation. Organic farming mandates that manure must first be composted or be used at least ninety days before harvest, which prevents bacteria from invading the food supply.
- Organic soil is better able to resist disease and insects naturally.
- Instead of insecticides, organic farmers use organisms in the soil, birds, insect predators, traps, barriers, and methods to disrupt insect mating. They apply certain natural pesticides only as a last resort.

Facts About Organic Farming and Sustainability

Researchers at McGill University in Montreal, Quebec, Canada, and at the University of Minnesota conducted a study analysis published in *Nature* in 2012. They analyzed sixty-six studies and concluded:

- Organic yields are lower than conventional yields;
- some organic crops have only 5 percent lower yields;
- there were 13 percent lower yields when best organic practices were used;
- in cases where conventional and organic practices were most similar, organics had 34 percent lower yields;
- because organic fields have lower yields than conventional fields, organic crops require more land and resources, causing more deforestation, loss of species, and other environmental harms; and
- a blend of organic and conventional farming will likely be required to produce affordable crops with low environmental impact.

According to the Organic Trade Association:

- Organic farmers have a primary goal to build healthy soil, which is the foundation of the food chain.

- Organic farming maintains a balanced and healthy ecosystem, feeds animals by growing forage crops, and retains wetlands and other natural areas.
- By not using polluting chemicals or releasing nitrogen into the water supply, organic farmers protect resources.
- Biodiversity, or preserving a wide variety of species, is important for a healthy environment. Many organic farmers support this by collecting and preserving unusual varieties of seeds.
- Organic farmers experiment, largely at their own expense, with reducing agriculture's impact on the environment.
- Even agricultural products that experts said could not be grown organically—like cotton—are now able to be.

According to the International Society for Ecology and Culture [ISEC], supporting local organic food has these benefits:

- It revitalizes rural communities by supporting small farms;
- it minimizes the need for pesticides, chemical fertilizers, preservatives, and packaging;
- it eliminates unnecessary food transportation, reducing fossil fuel use and pollution;
- it makes nutritious food more abundant and more affordable everywhere; and
- small organic farms are far more productive per acre than conventional farms.

The ISEC's recommendations to make local organic food accessible to all, including the poor, are:

- cut subsidies for conventional foods and give them to local markets instead;
- reduce government funding for biotechnology and pesticides and increase research that supports small organic farms;
- rather than subsidize long-distance shipping of foods, fund smaller community-based enterprises;
- increase prices of industrial foods, lower the price of local food; and tax fuels to reduce pollution; and
- regulate global corporations to discourage them from invading local markets.

Organizations to Contact

The editors have compiled the following list of organizations concerned with the issues debated in this book. The descriptions are derived from materials provided by the organizations. All have publications or information available for interested readers. The list was compiled on the date of publication of the present volume; the information provided here may change. Be aware that many organizations take several weeks or longer to respond to inquiries, so allow as much time as possible for the receipt of requested materials.

American Council on Science and Health (ACSH)
1995 Broadway, 2nd Fl.
New York, NY 10023-5860
(212) 362-7044
e-mail: acsh@acsh.org
website: www.acsh.org

The ACSH provides consumers with scientific evaluations of food and the environment, pointing out both health hazards and benefits. It participates in a variety of government and media events, from congressional hearings to popular magazines.

Campaign for Food Safety (CFS)
6101 Cliff Estate Rd.
Little Marais, MN 55614
(218) 226-4164
website: www.purefood.org

The CFS promotes the growth of organic and sustainable agriculture practices. CFS activist strategies include education, boycotts, grassroots lobbying, litigation, networking, direct action protests, and media events.

Cato Institute
1000 Massachusetts Ave. NW
Washington, DC 20001-5403

(202) 842-0200
fax: (202) 842-3490
e-mail: cato@cato.org
website: www.cato.org

The Cato Institute is a libertarian public policy research foundation dedicated to limiting the role of government and protecting individual liberties. It asserts that the concern over the possible health risks of pesticide use in agriculture is overstated. The institute publishes the quarterly *Cato Journal*, the bimonthly *Cato Policy Report*, and numerous books and commentaries.

Center for Science in the Public Interest (CSPI)
1220 L St. NW, Ste. 300
Washington, DC 20005
(202) 332-9110
e-mail: cspi@cspinet.org
website: www.cspinet.org

The CSPI is a nonprofit education and advocacy organization committed to improving the safety and nutritional quality of the US food supply.

Cornucopia Institute
PO Box 126
Cornucopia, WI 54827
(608) 625-2042
e-mail: cultivate@cornucopia.org
website: www.cornucopia.org

The Cornucopia Institute's mission is to promote economic justice for family-scale farming. It supports educational activities that spread the ecological principles and economic wisdom that underlay sustainable and organic agriculture. Through research and investigations on agricultural issues, the institute provides information to consumers, family farmers, and the media about organic food and farming.

Food First Institute for Food and Development Policy
398 Sixtieth St.
Oakland, CA 94618
(510) 654-4400
website: www.foodfirst.org

Food First, founded by the author of *Diet for a Small Planet*, promotes sustainable agriculture. Its current projects include the Cuban Organic Agriculture Exchange Program and Californians for Pesticide Reform.

Food Safety Consortium (FSC)
110 Agriculture Bldg.
University of Arkansas
Fayetteville, AR 72701
(501) 575-5647
website: www.uark.edu/depts/fsc

Congress established the FSC, consisting of researchers from the University of Arkansas, Iowa State University, and Kansas State University, in 1988 through a special Cooperative State Research Service grant. The FSC conducts extensive investigation into all areas of poultry, beef, and pork meat production.

Friends of the Earth (FoE)
1100 Fifteenth St. NW, 11th Fl.
Washington, DC 20005
(202) 783-7400
e-mail: foe@foe.org
website: www.foe.org

The FoE monitors legislation and regulations that affect the environment. Its Safer Food, Safer Farms Campaign speaks out against what it perceives as the negative impact that biotechnology can have on farming, food production, genetic resources, and the environment.

Organic Consumers Association
6771 S. Silver Hill Dr.
Finland, MN 55603
(218) 226-4164
website: www.organicconsumers.org

This grassroots nonprofit public interest organization campaigns for health, justice, and sustainability. It deals with issues of food safety, industrial agriculture, genetic engineering, children's health, corporate accountability, fair trade, environmental sustainability, and other key topics. It is the only organization in the United States focused exclusively on promoting the views and interests of the nation's estimated 50 million organic and socially responsible consumers.

Organic Farming Research Foundation (OFRF)
303 Potrero St., Ste. 29-203
Santa Cruz, CA 95060
website: http://ofrf.org

OFRF conducts original research about organic farming in the United States. Since 1992 the organization has conducted four National Organic Farmers' Surveys, collecting information about organic farmers' research and information needs, their experiences in the organic marketplace, effects of genetically modified organisms on organic production and markets, organic farmer demographics, and more.

Organic Materials Review Institute (OMRI)
2649 Willamette St.
Eugene, OR 97405-3134
(541) 343-7600
website: www.omri.org

This national nonprofit organization determines which input products are allowed for use in organic production and processing. OMRI Listed® products are allowed for use in certified organic operations under the US Department of Agriculture's National Organic Program. The organization's website features a useful database visitors can use to find organic products.

Organic Trade Association (OTA)
PO Box 547
Greenfield, MA 01302
(413) 774-7511
website: www.ota.com

The OTA is a membership-based business association that focuses on the organic business community in North America. The OTA's mission is to promote and protect the growth of organic trade to benefit the environment, farmers, the public, and the economy.

Rodale Institute
611 Siegfriedale Rd.
Kutztown, PA 19530-9320
(610) 683-1400
e-mail: info@rodaleinst.org
website: www.rodaleinstitute.org

The Rodale Institute was founded in 1947 by organic pioneer J.I. Rodale. The institute employs soil scientists and a cooperating network of researchers who document how organic farming techniques offer the best solution to global warming and famine. Its website offers information on the longest-running US study comparing organic and conventional farming techniques, which is the basis for Rodale's practical training to thousands of farmers in Africa, Asia, and the Americas.

US Department of Agriculture (USDA)
1400 Independence Ave. SW
Washington, DC 20250
website: www.usda.gov

This government organization is charged with regulating the standards for any farm, wild crop harvesting, or handling operation that wants to sell an agricultural product as organically produced. The USDA has set requirements for the importing and exporting of organic products. More information about this process is available on its website, as are numerous fact sheets and publications about the state of food in America.

US Environmental Protection Agency (EPA)
Ariel Rios Bldg.
1200 Pennsylvania Ave. NW
Washington, DC 20460
(202) 272-0167
website: www.epa.gov

The EPA is a government agency that regulates pesticides under two major federal statutes. It establishes maximum legally permissible levels for pesticide residues in food, registers pesticides for use in the United States, and prescribes labeling and other regulatory requirements to prevent unreasonable adverse effects on health or the environment.

US Food and Drug Administration (FDA)
10903 New Hampshire Ave.
Silver Spring, MD 20903
(888) 463-6332
website: www.fda.gov

The FDA is the public health agency charged with protecting American consumers by enforcing the Federal Food, Drug, and Cosmetic Act and several related public health laws. To carry out this mandate of consumer protection, the FDA has investigators and inspectors cover the country's almost ninety-five thousand FDA-regulated businesses. Its publications include government documents, reports, fact sheets, and press announcements.

For Further Reading

Books

Gillman, Jeff. *The Truth About Organic Gardening: Benefits, Drawbacks, and the Bottom Line.* Portland, OR: Timber, 2008. Challenges assumptions that organic products are automatically safe for humans and beneficial to the environment.

Hewitt, Ben. *The Town That Food Saved: How One Community Found Vitality in Local Food.* Emmaus, PA: Rodale, 2011. Traces the story of Hardwick, Vermont, a hardscrabble farming community that jump-started its economy and redefined its self-image through a local, self-sustaining food system.

Kaufman, Frederick. *Bet the Farm: How Food Stopped Being Food.* Hoboken, NJ: Wiley, 2012. Explores the connection between the global food system and why the food on our tables is getting less healthy and less delicious even as the world's biggest food companies and food scientists say things are better than ever.

Nestle, Marion. *Eat Drink Vote: An Illustrated Guide to Food Politics.* Emmaus, PA: Rodale, 2013. This renowned foodie presents more than 250 of her favorite cartoons on issues ranging from dietary advice to genetic engineering to organic food and farming.

Nestle, Marion, and Michael Pollan. *Food Politics: How the Food Industry Influences Nutrition and Health.* Berkeley: University of California Press, 2013. Explains how much the food industry influences government nutrition policies and how cleverly it links its interests to those of nutrition experts.

Paarlberg, Robert. *Food Politics: What Everyone Needs to Know.* New York: Oxford University Press, 2010. Examines numerous issues regarding today's global food landscape, including international food prices, famines, chronic hunger, the Malthusian race between food production and population growth, international food aid, "green revolution" farming, obesity, farm subsidies and trade, agriculture and the environment, agribusiness, supermarkets, food safety, fast food, slow food, organic food, local food, and genetically engineered food.

Reed, Matthew. *Rebels for the Soil: The Rise of the Global Organic Food and Farming Movement.* New York: Routledge, 2010. Investigates the emergence of organic food and farming as a social movement, explaining how both people and ideas have shaped a movement that from its inception aimed to change global agriculture.

Rodale, Maria. *Organic Manifesto: How Organic Food Can Heal Our Planet, Feed the World, and Keep Us Safe.* Emmaus, PA: Rodale, 2011. Drawing on findings from leading health researchers as well as conversations with both chemical and organic farmers, the author outlines the unacceptably high cost of chemical farming on our health and our environment.

Ronald, Pamela C., and R.W. Adamchak. *Tomorrow's Table: Organic Farming, Genetics, and the Future of Food.* New York: Oxford University Press, 2010. Argues that a judicious blend of two important strands of agriculture—genetic engineering and organic farming—is key to helping feed the world's growing population in an ecologically balanced manner.

Periodicals

Bawden, Tom. "Organic Farming Hits the Skids as Recession-Hit Consumers Desert the Sector," *Independent* (London), June 16, 2013. www.independent.co.uk/environment/green-living/organ ic-farming-hits-the-skids-as-recessionhit-consumers-desert-the -sector-8660916.html.

Benbrook, Charles, Urvashi Rangan, and Jeffrey Steingarten. "Organic Food Is Marketing Hype," *Intelligence Squared U.S.*, April 13, 2010. www.organic-center.org/reportfiles/Debate_Transcript.pdf.

Biello, David. "Will Organic Food Fail to Feed the World?," *Scientific American*, April 25, 2012. www.scientificamerican.com/article .cfm?id=organic-farming-yields-and-feeding-the-world-under -climate-change.

Block, John R. "A Reality Check for Organic Food Dreamers," *Wall Street Journal*, December 23, 2012. http://online.wsj.com/article /SB10001424127887323297104578174963239598312.html.

Bowden, Jonny. "The Organic Food Lie," *Huffington Post*, September 12, 2012. www.huffingtonpost.com/dr-jonny-bowden/the-organic -food-lie_b_1866043.html.

Brown, Elizabeth Nolan. "Ignore the Hype—Organic Food Is Still Better for You," Blisstree, September 4, 2012. www.blisstree .com/2012/09/04/food/nutrition/why-you-should-ignore-the -organic-food-isnt-healthier-hype-592.

Carroll, Aaron. "Healthy Food Doesn't Mean 'Organic,'" CNN, September 11, 2012. www.cnn.com/2012/09/11/opinion/carroll -organic-food.

Fung, Brian. "Organic Food Isn't More Nutritious, But That Isn't the Point," *Atlantic*, September 4, 2012. www.theatlantic.com/health /archive/2012/09/organic-food-isnt-more-nutritious-but-that-isnt -the-point/261929.

Greenaway, Twilight. "Organic Food: Still More than an Elitist Lifestyle Choice," *Grist*, September 10, 2012. http://grist.org/food /organic-food-still-more-than- an-elitist-lifestyle-choice.

Hurst, Blake. "Organic Illusions," *American*, October 1, 2012. www .american.com/archive/2012/october/organic-illusions.

Los Angeles Times, "The Case for Organic Food," September 5, 2012. http://articles.latimes.com/2012/sep/05/opinion/la-ed-organ ics-20120905.

McGuire, Peter. "Organic Food: A Waste of Money," *Huffington Post*, November 2, 2013. www.huffingtonpost.co.uk/peter-mcguire /organic-food-waste-of- money_b_2638840.html.

Miller, Henry I., and Richard Cornett. "Is Organic Agriculture 'Affluent Narcissism?,'" *Forbes*, November 7, 2012. www.forbes .com/sites/henrymiller/2012/11/07/organic-agricultures-bitter -taste-or-is-organic-agriculture-affluent-narcissism.

Popoff, Mischa. "How Safe Is Your Organic Food?," Committee for a Constructive Tomorrow, June 19, 2013. www.cfact.org /2013/06/19/how-safe- is-your-organic-food.

Shiffman, Richard. "Only Organics Can Feed the Hungry World: Here's Why," Truthout, October 13, 2012. http://truth-out.org /opinion/item/12018-only-organics- can-feed-the-hungry-world -heres-why.

Stout, Andrew. "Challenging the 'Conventional' Wisdom: One Farmer's Take on the Stanford Organic Food Study," *Huffington Post*, September 21, 2012. www.huffingtonpost.com/andrew-stout /farmer-stanford-organic- study_b_1901677.html.

Walston, Oliver. "Organic Farming Just Doesn't Earn Its Corn," *Telegraph* (London), June 9, 2010. www.telegraph.co.uk/earth /agriculture/geneticmodification/7814598/Organic-farming-just -doesnt-earn-its-corn.html.

Websites

Local Harvest (www.localharvest.org). This website allows users to find locally grown produce anywhere in the country. The interactive map allows people to locate farmers' markets, family farms, community-supported agriculture (CSA), farm stands, and you-pick farms in their area.

Mark's Daily Apple (www.marksdailyapple.com). This site run by Mark Sisson offers information on health, nutrition, fitness, the health industry, and the low-carb primal lifestyle. Sisson frequently weighs in on topics related to organic food and farming.

On Food (http://bittman.blogs.nytimes.com). Food columnist Mark Bittman writes this blog for the *New York Times*. He frequently covers topics pertaining to organic food and farming.

Organic.org (www.organic.org). In addition to featuring numerous articles and fact sheets about organic food and farming, this site has a useful interactive map visitors can use to find stores near them that carry organic products.

Sustainable Table (www.sustainabletable.org). This website promotes sustainable food and farming, rather than strictly organically grown products.

Index

London School of Hygiene and Tropical Medicine, 41
Los Angeles Times (newspaper), 49
Lunder, Sonya, 36, 39

M
Mancozeb, human toxicity/ecotoxicity, 20
Manure, requirement for organic farmers to compost, 37
Mark, Jason, 12
Mastio, David, 29
McMahon, Beth, 46–47, 73–75
McWilliams, James, 82
Meats, antibiotic-resistant bacteria on, 47
Media, reporting on toxic substances by, 27
Melchett, Peter, 42
Monsanto, 37, 52

N
Naked Economics (Wheelen), 55
National Agricultural Statistics Service (NASS), 83–85
National Farmers Union (UK), 44
National Organics Program (NOP), 103–106
National Research Council, 79
Nature (journal), 72, 73
Nestle, Marion, 77, 81
New York Times (newspaper), 13
No-till farming, 60

NOP (National Organics Program), 103–106

O
Opinion polls. *See* Surveys
Orbach, Martin, 93
Organic Center, 42
Organic certification/labeling, 92—93
  guidelines for, *106*
  is not based on strict requirements, 108–112
  as reason to charge more, opinion on, *26*
  requirements for, 102–107
Organic cooperatives, 7–8
Organic farming
  can feed the world, 76–81
  cannot feed the world, 82–87
  conserves resources, 65–70
  energy use in, *vs.* conventional systems, 54, *69, 70*
  is environmentally friendly, 51–57, 91–92
  is not environmentally friendly, 47–48, 58–64
  reduces exposure to toxic chemicals, 12–17
  requires more land than conventional farming, 62, 71–75
Organic Farming Research Foundation, 37
Organic foods
  are elitist, 89–94
  are not elitist, 95–101

are not prone to
contamination by
pathogens, 35–39
are prone to contamination
by pathogens, 29–34
lower pesticide residues are
not a good reason to buy,
18–28
may be higher in nutrients
than conventional food,
40–44, 96
reduces exposure to toxic
chemicals, 12–17
sales of, 90, *100*
The Organic Green Revolution
(Rodale Institute), 79–80
Organic Manifesto (Rodale), *53*
Organic Trade Association,
30–31, 68, 90
Organophosphate pesticides,
23–24
impacts on children, 15
Other Avenues Food
Cooperative, 7–9

P
Palmer, Brian, 65
Pesticide Data Program
(PDP, US Department of
Agriculture), 21–22
Pesticide drift, 36
Pesticide(s)
estimated amount used in US
agriculture, 56
organic crops require more
than conventional crops, 62
organic food/farming reduces
exposure to, 12–17, 62

residue in conventionally
grown fruits/vegetables,
16
small doses of, may be
beneficial, 24
synthetic, energy use for,
68
Pineapples, *78*
Pollan, Michael, 77, 81
Polls. *See* Surveys
Popoff, Mischa, 108
Pyrethrum, 20

R
Rainbow Grocery co-op, 8–9
Rapeseed crop, *84*
Reduced Risk Program
(Environmental Protection
Agency), 20
Rodale, Maria, 51
Rodale Institute, 52, 67, *67*,
79–80
Rotenone, 20–21, 23

S
Salatin, Joel, 95, *99*
Salmonella, in organic *vs.*
conventional foods, 33
Savage, Steve, 58, 83, 84, 85,
87
Seufert, Verena, 73
Sexton, Steve, 77
Smallwood, Mark, 68
Solomon, Zak, 102
Soupcoff, Marni, 45
Soybeans, average yields for
conventional *vs.* organic
crops, *80*

Picture Credits

© ableimages/Alamy, 38

© AgStock Images, Inc./Alamy, 84

© AP Images/Markus Schreiber, 31

© AP Images/Rick Smith, 67

© BSIP/UIG via Getty Images, 78

© Enigma/Alamy, 11

© Gale, Cengage, 16, 26, 32, 43, 63, 69, 74, 80, 86, 100, 106

© Bill Hogan/Chicago Tribune/MCT via Getty Images, 53

© Robert Nickelsberg/Getty Images, 50

© José Antonio Peňas/Science Source, 21

© Chuck Place/Alamy, 48

© redbrickstock.com/Alamy, 15

© Steve Russell/Toronto Star via Getty Images, 111

© Ilya S. Savenok/Getty Images, 99

© Science Source, 61

© Brendon Thorne/Bloomberg via Getty Images, 91

© Nick Turner/Alamy, 88